Whistleblower Doctor

The Politics and Economics
Of Pain and Dying

David K. Cundiff, MD

Also by David K. Cundiff, MD

Euthanasia is Not the Answer—A Hospice Physician's View

The Right Medicine—How Make Health Care Reform Work Today

Money Driven Medicine—Tests and Treatments That Don't Work

The Health Economy

All available at: http://TheHealthEconomy.com/

Library of Congress Cataloging in Publication Data
Cundiff, David K.
> Whistleblower Doctor—The Politics and Economics of Pain and Dying
> David K. Cundiff
> ISBN 0-9761571-3-6
> 1. Medical care—United States.
> 2. Hospice—United States.
> 3. Health Care Reform—United States.
> 4. Health care economics—United States.
> 5. Medical malpractice reform—United States
> 6. Cancer and AIDS pain management
> 7. Anticoagulation prophylaxis and treatment

DEDICATED

with much respect
to

To the patients and staff of the LA County + USC
Medical Center, who deserve to receive and
deliver the best possible medical care.

Contents*

* This book is documented with 422 appendices and 44 exhibits
totaling over 2,000 pages. To access any appendix or exhibit online,
go to http://TheHealthEconomy.com/WD/Appendices.htm and
click on the appropriate appendix or exhibit.

Executive Summary

A one-month experience of working in three hospices in England convinced me to focus my medical career on alleviating pain and suffering of terminally ill cancer patients. After finishing my fellowship training in hematology and medical oncology (cancer) at the University of California San Diego Medical Center, I resolved to find a way of integrating hospice principles and philosophy with my practice of cancer medicine.

I worked at the Los Angeles County Department of Health Services (LAC-DHS) from 1979–1998, including nine years of directing the Pain and Palliative Care Service at the Los Angeles County+University of Southern California Medical Center (LAC+USC Medical Center). By the early 1990s, the Pain and Palliative Care Service (the Service) had become very popular with the patients, housestaff, nurses, social workers, and other caregivers. Overworked residents and nurses saw that we alleviated pain of their patients while reducing work for the hospital caregivers. We provided their patients with outpatient hospice follow-up and 24-hour/seven-day phone availability that prevented many readmissions for uncontrolled symptoms. In addition, we educated the doctors and nurses in pain management and palliative care techniques.

Unfortunately, for the financial bottom line of the hospital, the better the Service controlled pain and distressing symptoms the more money the hospital lost. Our success in controlling pain and providing comfort to over 400 terminally ill patients led to an estimated 4,000 fewer reimbursable inpatient days in 1994, saving the taxpayer over $9 million in Medi-Cal spending. (California's Medicaid program) However, LAC-DHS management did not appreciate the savings to taxpayers by the Service, since our efficient and effective outpatient care reduced the Medical Center's revenue by the same $9 million.

By the time cancer and AIDS patients reached the end stages of their diseases, they almost all had Medi-Cal insurance. Consequently, prolonged hospitalizations for terminally ill cancer and AIDS patients served as a "cash cow" for the LAC+USC Medical Center. This population comprised less than 1% of patients treated, but yielded as much as 15% of the $700 million Medi-Cal yearly revenue for the Medical Center. Since Medi-Cal paid a high all-inclusive daily fee for acute hospital care and little for outpatient treatment, the LAC+USC Medical Center needed a high inpatient census to maximize government reimbursement for services. This discouraged appropriate outpatient pain management and palliative care for terminally ill cancer and AIDS patients.

As the Service had an increasingly adverse effect on inpatient census, management became more and more hostile to me. They reassigned me to additional duties, took away two federal grants for improving the evaluation and treatment of pain, did not permit me to apply for other outside funds to improve pain management, and failed to allocate resources to keep up with the volume of work.

Financial Crisis Hits LAC-DHS

In the summer of 1995, the LAC-DHS faced the largest budget shortfall in its history—$655 million deficit out of an operating budget of $2.3 billion. To resolve the budget crisis, the Los Angeles County Chief Administrative Officer's proposed budget to the Board of Supervisors for 1995–96 included the closure of the LAC+USC Medical Center. After all of the politicians and County Administrators completed their negotiations over the crisis, the LAC+USC Medical Center was saved, but employees and services of the LAC-DHS were downsized by nearly 15%. Under the cover of this crisis, the LAC-USC Medical Center management closed the Pain and Palliative Care Service and transferred me to attending in internal medicine inpatient wards and outpatient clinics.

In conjunction with the LAC-DHS downsizing of personnel and services in September 1995, management negotiated a $1.2 billion five-year Health Department bailout from President Clinton to save the LA County Government from threatened bankruptcy. The strings attached to the bailout included reengineering the LAC-DHS to shift considerable resources from inpatient care to out-of-hospital services. I rejoiced that, finally, financial sanity would come to the LAC-DHS and that pain management and palliative care would have to be recognized as a necessary component to comprehensive care, requiring significant resources.

Inexplicably, the federal Medicaid bureaucracy increased rather than decreased our inpatient reimbursement rate and did not increase funding for outpatient services. I had hoped for a comprehensive change in the system of funding the LAC-DHS to per patient (capitated) reimbursement or another system that encouraged outpatient care. Paradoxically, complying with the conditions of the federal bailout by shifting resources from inpatient to outpatient care would have severely reduced revenues to the LAC-DHS. Consequently, resources were never shifted.

Challenging the LA County+USC Medical Center $900 Million Replacement Project

After averting the Medical Center closure by receiving the federal bailout in 1995 and securing an outrageous daily fee rate for Medi-Cal inpatients ($3,800 per day), LAC-DHS management next set its sights on replacing the aging Medical Center with as large a hospital as possible. The more beds in the new hospital, the more of the 8,300 LAC+USC Medical Center employees would salvage their jobs. This increased ongoing census-raising strategies that precluded an effective pain and palliative care service designed to help terminally ill patients remain comfortably at home rather than in acute-care hospital beds.

Policies and procedures throughout the Medical Center encouraged unnecessary hospitalizations and encouraged more days in hospital than needed for those admitted appropriately. Major deficiencies in primary care services in affiliated clinics and comprehensive health care centers paid off financially with more emergency admissions to the hospital. As had long been the case at LAC-DHS hospitals, admitted patients could wait days or weeks for surgery, diagnostic studies, or specialty medical procedures. Nearly everyone believed that the long waits were due to underfunding of the LAC-DHS. In reality, the LAC-DHS depended on long waits of Medi-Cal patients to increase revenue. Inefficiency paid well while efficiency was financially punished.

In a highly contentious meeting in November 1997, the LA County Board of Supervisors approved a 600-bed replacement hospital instead of the management-supported proposal of 750 beds. This meant that up to 4,000 jobs would be lost at the Medical Center.

Later that month I published an editorial in the *LA Times*, advocating that the LAC-DHS lease acute-care hospital beds from private hospitals or buy existing hospitals instead of spending $900 million on a replacement hospital. Since LA County had about 20,000 acute-care licensed beds, of which only about 10,000 were filled in an average day, I argued that a replacement hospital of any size would waste taxpayers' money. Instead, I recommended immediately switching to per patient (capitated) reimbursement from Medi-Cal, reorganizing the LAC-DHS as a health maintenance organization, and leasing or buying the necessary acute-care beds from the private sector. Then, we could effectively compete with the rest of the LA community health care providers by making efficient use of hospital beds and shifting more resources to out-of-hospital care, such as hospice. With capitated reimbursement, we would no longer be financially dependent on institutionalized inefficiency and waste driven by the dysfunctional funding system.

Management responded to my editorial with resounding silence. Despite the fact that I claimed that the Health Department fostered dysfunctional policies and procedures that purposefully raised the census solely to increase reimbursement, no one issued a verbal or written rebuttal.

In February 1998, I audited my inpatient medical service, carefully documenting the unnecessary patient days in hospital. Applying my findings to the census figures of the LAC+USC Medical Center, I calculated that the average inpatient census should have been about 480 patients rather than the actual 860 (44% of days unnecessary). In March 1998, I sent the results of this audit and my suggestions for re-engineering the LAC-DHS to the federal and California State Medicaid offices and to 11 legislators. Only the California State Medi-Cal office replied to the conclusion from my audit that the Medical Center was defrauding Medi-Cal out of over $200 million per year by institutionalized inefficiencies. They did nothing to investigate.

Chief among these strategies to raise the inpatient census was inadequate pain management and palliative care services, accounting for 28% of the unnecessary inpatient days in my audit.

Complaints about Poor Treatment of 83 Patients

After the Pain and Palliative Care Service closed in September 1995, I assumed full-time duties as an attending physician on the general medicine wards and in the outpatient clinics. In those roles I found numerous instances of poor pain and symptom management of cancer and AIDS patients. Over five years I submitted 83 incident reports to the LAC+USC Quality Assurance Committee, mostly about patients suffering poor pain management. I also formally submitted these cases as patient care complaints to the Medical Board of California. The Medical Center QA Committee did not acknowledge receipt of the complaints. The Medical Board responded that the patients and/or patients' families would have to submit the complaints rather than a physician that was aware of the substandard care. Unfortunately, all the patients were dead and I had no access to the charts at that point to contact the families.

Fired and Medical License Revoked

Four days after I sent the results of my inpatient service audit to Medicaid administrators in Washington, DC and Sacramento and several legislators, my supervisor placed me on paid administrative leave. Seven months later management fired me supposedly for my clinical decision (a judgment call) to stop the drug Coumadin (generic name: warfarin, a blood thinner) in an alcoholic patient with a leg clot (deep venous thrombosis or DVT). He had a very high bleeding risk. The patient later died of a clot in his lung. I had no previous malpractice judgments or disciplinary actions in 25 years of practice.

In a Civil Service Hearing, I lost my case to be reinstated in my job. Subsequently, the California Superior Court denied my appeal. Finally, I faced a California State Medical Board hearing for my medical license.

I defended my judgment to stop the Coumadin in my patient by pointing out that Coumadin is contraindicated in alcoholic patients because of the bleeding risk. My medical resident on the case diagnosed alcoholism by documenting in the chart that the patient reported drinking a six-pack of beer per day for 20 years. Neither the Deputy Attorney General nor the judge disputed that alcoholism is a contraindication for using Coumadin for deep venous thrombosis. The decision in the case hung on whether the patient was an alcoholic.

The Deputy Attorney General responded by bringing the patient's daughter to the stand in court as a surprise witness to testify not only about her account of the events of her father's illness but also as a quasi expert witness. She worked as a substance abuse counselor. She said that her father did not drink "cans of beer" but "quart bottles of Colt 45 Malt Liquor"—not more than two quarts of malt liquor per day on weekends. She testified that she had never seen her father drunk and that he was not an alcoholic. The district attorney brought no other substance abuse expert witnesses to challenge the diagnosis of alcoholism documented in the chart by my medical resident who, under cross examination, stood firmly by the accuracy of her medical history.

Referring to the daughter's testimony, Administrative Law Judge H. Stuart Waxman wrote in his decision to revoke my medical license, ". . . (The patient) drank less than two quarts of malt liquor per day on weekends. (The evidence did not disclose his drinking customs during his workweek.)" Rejecting my defense that it would have been malpractice for me to continue the Coumadin in an alcoholic, Judge Waxman ruled that I should have continued the Coumadin.

He would not allow into evidence the results of a survey of internists and anticoagulation experts done by my expert witness, Dr. Matthew Conolly, UCLA Professor of Medicine, and me that showed a remarkable variation of medical opinion about the best management of the case. After hearing my testimony on the lack of scientific evidence supporting anticoagulant treatment of deep venous thrombosis, Judge Waxman asked me that were I to treat another patient with identical circumstances, would I again stop the Coumadin. I said, "Yes."

In his decision on my case, Judge Waxman wrote:

> ". . . Respondent is now even more convinced than he was in 1998 that he made the correct decision in discontinuing the anticoagulant medication he had been approving for (patient) BR, and he made it very clear at the administrative hearing that, if faced with the same situation today, he would make the exact same decision. Respondent is entitled to that opinion. However, he is not entitled to foist that opinion on an unsuspecting public, more than 2,000,000 of whom suffer DVT annually. Those popliteal DVT patients who may be treated by Respondent in the future are now at even greater risk of pulmonary embolism than before because of Respondent's ongoing belief that the

standard treatment for the condition, accepted by the vast majority of the medical profession, is nothing more than "dogma." No probationary order can adequately address and prevent that risk to the public. That risk to the public is too great to permit Respondent's continued practice of medicine."

After I lost my medical license over this case, the patient's daughter brought a wrongful death civil suit against me and LA County, which the County administration settled, over my objections, for $175,000. In a deposition of the patient's daughter before the settlement, my attorney showed her a 40-ounce magnum of Colt 45 Malt Liquor, asking if this was her father's preferred drink. After she said it was, she acknowledged her error in calling it a quart (32 ounces). Two magnums of malt liquor are equivalent in alcohol to eight 12-ounce cans of beer. Only an alcoholic with a high tolerance could consume this much in a day and not appear drunk.

Discovering that Anticoagulation Increases Deaths Overall

This DVT case led me to research the evidence-basis for warfarin (Coumadin) and other anticoagulants for treating clots in the leg and lung veins (DVTs and pulmonary emboli or PE, together called venous thromboembolism or VTE). To my great surprise, I found all the published studies supporting anticoagulants for DVT and PE to be flawed. In court, my expert witness, Dr. Conolly, and I testified about a particular randomized controlled clinical trial comparing standard anticoagulants (heparin and warfarin) to phenylbutazone (an anti-inflammatory drug). The prosecuting attorney objected to us entering the trial into evidence, and the judge sustained the objection. In malpractice proceedings, you cannot have expert witnesses debate the evidence-basis of a medical test or treatment. All that matters is the prevailing opinion of the medical establishment.

I have subsequently published a number of articles in peer-reviewed medical journals showing that anticoagulants increase rather than decrease mortality for deep venous thrombosis. I found that 28 other medical indications for anticoagulants to be likewise based on scientific errors and biases of drug company-funded investigators. None of these challenges to "standard" anticoagulant treatment has been rebutted by any anticoagulation expert in academia or government.

Worldwide, at least 100,000 people bleed to death from anticoagulants or die of rebound clotting after stopping anticoagulants each year. My quest is to stop this doctor-caused epidemic.

Stonewalling of U.S. Department of Health Services Health Regulators

In August 2010, my sixth major review article challenging the effectiveness and safety of anticoagulation was published by a BioMed Central Journal. (http://www.tbiomed.com/content/7/1/31) The article entitled, "Diet for prophylaxis and treatment of venous thromboembolism?", reviewed the data on anticoagulation drugs for prophylaxis and treatment of VTE and found that they cause about 40,000 deaths per year worldwide of which about 20,000 occur in the U.S. The article went on to recommend either withdrawing the FDA approval of anticoagulants for VTE or funding randomized controlled clinical trials to compare a low VTE risk diet (mostly plant-based foods) with standard anticoagulation for VTE.

I immediately notified leaders at the Food and Drug Administration (FDA) and National Institutes of Health (NIH) by email of the publication of this article and requested their critique. Janet Woodcock, MD, Director of the Center for Drug Research and Evaluation of the FDA, delegated the job of replying to me to Ann Farrell, MD, Acting Director of the FDA Division of Hematology Products. Dr. Farrell was explicit about refusing to go on record with a critique of my paper: "We have reviewed your interesting paper but have no written critique."

My email to Francis Collins, MD, Director of the NIH began

> I am the lead author of an article published in a BioMed Central Journal that provided literature documentation that anticoagulant prophylaxis and treatment for venous thromboembolism (VTE, i.e., DVT and PE) unnecessarily causes about 40,000 bleeding and rebound clotting deaths per year worldwide, about 20,000 of which occur in the U.S. http://www.tbiomed.com/content/7/1/31 . . .

Dr. Collins delegated his reply to me to Susan Shurin, MD, Acting Director National Heart, Lung, and Blood Institute. Dr. Shurin completely avoided any direct response to my data and conclusions of the article and replied in boilerplate bureaucratese:

> The risks and benefits of the prophylactic and therapeutic use of current anticoagulation therapies are well recognized. Therefore, the NHLBI actively supports basic, translational, and clinical research on safer and more effective therapeutic options for VTE. . . .

Despite multiple attempts by me and others to have FDA and NIH scientists and drug regulators critique the data and conclusions of this article of any of my other five published peer-reviewed medical journal articles showing that anticoagulants do catastrophic harm to people, they continue to stonewall with no public, transparent, detailed analysis of my data and conclusions.

Medical License Reinstatement Hearing in LA County Superior Court

On May 27, 2011, I will appear before Judge James Chalfant in Los Angeles County Superior Court to appeal for the reinstatement of my medical license. Deputy Attorney General Klint McKay's brief in opposition to my license reinstatement maintains that I am a risk to patients because of my opinion that anticoagulant drugs do harm in patients with deep venous thrombosis.

My reply brief concludes:

> Petitioner's medical judgment that anticoagulants for VTE treatment increase the risk of death has not been rebutted in six peer-reviewed medical articles published from 2004–2010. That anticoagulants cause catastrophic harm to patients has not been rebutted by the FDA or NIH leaders in charge of regulating these drugs. The burden is on Respondent to produce declarations by authoritative physicians that are expert in anticoagulation medicine to address

Petitioner's medical judgment in 2011 that
anticoagulant medication for treatment of VTE does
harm to patients. Failing that, Respondent should
reinstate Petitioner's medical license.

Conclusion

By relating my 19-year saga in the LAC-DHS, I hope to focus
attention on issues that are much more important than my case for
medical license reinstatement:

1. My hostile work environment and job termination resulted
    from perverse financial incentives in the Medicaid program
    that rewarded hospitalization and discouraged outpatient
    hospice care. This increased pain and suffering and impaired
    training of health care providers, compounding the other
    barriers to effective and compassionate palliative care of the
    dying.
2. Anticoagulation drugs for VTE prophylaxis and treatment
    doesn't work and causes about 40,000 deaths per year
    worldwide. Drug company financial clout has exerted its
    influence on academic researchers, medical journal editors,
    government regulators, and the medical media to foster this
    ineffective, dangerous, and expensive practice.
3. For many other medical indications where anticoagulation is
    used according to clinical practice guidelines as the standard of
    care, it is not evidence-based to work and, in fact, may be
    evidence-based to increase complications and death.
4. "Sham peer-review," as in my case, has become an increasing
    problem that stifles health care innovation, efficiency, and
    quality of care improvement. Whistleblowing physicians who
    point out deficiencies in health care and expert physicians who
    pose competitive threats to local medical establishments may
    be targeted for retaliation like I was. Resolving the current
    medico-legal mess regarding physician malpractice requires a
    comprehensive overall of the tort system in health care.

More broadly, health care in the U.S. is in crisis with decreasing
access and quality while costs escalate. We will never be able to

control medical costs and provide universal access to quality medical care until we stop paying for tests and treatments that don't work such as anticoagulation drugs for prophylaxis and treatment of VTE. My saga relates to the need for a wide-based restructuring of health care to get the financial incentives right. If we properly reward good, efficient, compassionate care rather than ineffective medical interventions, quality will go up and costs will come down.

Chapter 1

Need for Pain Control
and Hospice Services

President Richard Nixon signed the National Cancer Act of 1971, providing generous funding to greatly expand the National Cancer Institute in order to cure cancer. Nixon wanted to outdo President John F. Kennedy who signed the legislation to put a man on the moon. As a third year medical student at the University of California, San Diego (UCSD) in 1971, I saw how dying cancer patients were neglected and decided to specialize in cancer treatment—medical oncology. After medical internship and residency at the University of Pittsburgh Hospitals, I took a fellowship in medical oncology at the Cancer Control Agency of British Columbia.

Many of my patients died horrible painful deaths despite my best efforts to cure them or alleviate their pain and suffering. No expert in pain management or hospice was available to call on for help. In my subsequent hematology (blood)-oncology fellowship at UCSD, my teachers, colleagues, and I focused on attempts to cure people or prolong life more than to relieve pain and distressing symptoms in people with advanced cancer. Again, no consultation service in cancer pain management was available for us to call for help.

To learn more about pain control and symptom management for cancer patients, I took my last clinical elective of my hematology-oncology fellowship in hospices in the United Kingdom. In 1979, over the course of one month, I served as assistant physician on hospice teams in London, Oxford, and Worthing. During that time, I participated in the care of over 100 cancer patients. Only one had poor pain control, and the morphine dose for that patient was still in the process of being adjusted. The superior quality of symptomatic care that these cancer patients received astounded me.

I was also amazed at my lack of knowledge of how to effectively prescribe medication to control the symptoms of the terminally ill. Previous to my experience in England, I literally did not know that I did not know how to effectively treat pain and distressing symptoms of advanced cancer. In some cases, a junior doctor only one year out of medical school taught me techniques of adjusting doses of morphine and related medicines—things I had not learned in six years of post graduate training in internal medicine and medical oncology. The English hospice consultants, nurses, and social workers showed me a manner of caring for patients that I could not have learned by reading books or attending lectures. They masterfully translated hospice philosophy and treatment knowledge into practical techniques to address the complex physical, psychological, social, and spiritual issues in order to help patients live fully and comfortably for whatever time their diseases allotted.

At the end of the experience, I resolved to bring this quality holistic care for the terminally ill—palliating the physical, psychological, social, and spiritual suffering—to whatever type of oncology practice I would subsequently undertake. My perspective on medicine and on life was forever changed.

LA County+USC Medical Center Hospice Care/Pain Management Subcommittee

Before disbanding in 1984, the Los Angeles County-Department of Health Services (LAC-DHS) Ad Hoc Committee on Hospice recommended to the LA County Board of Supervisors that the County should start a hospice program and appoint a full-time hospice and pain control physician for the Department of Health Services. Consequently, in 1985, the Hospice Care/Pain Management Subcommittee of the Quality Assurance Committee was formed at the LAC+USC Medical Center in response to the request of the LAC-DHS that each County hospital review care of the dying and the facility's approach to pain control in cancer patients. Because of my interest and work in this area, the hospital medical director appointed me to this subcommittee.

On May 24, 1985, Peter Heseltine, MD, Chairman, of the Quality Assurance (QA) Committee, and Kathy Lohr, RN, Coordinator of the QA Committee, reported that, "Considering our findings, as well as those of the LAC-DHS Ad Hoc Committee on Hospice, we feel that the lack of medical training in pain control and palliative care is an epidemic problem." (Appendix #3) On August 23, 1985, the Committee minutes stated the following: (Appendix #4)

2

The committee indicated that the first goal should be to make people realize that there is a problem with pain management. Although the committee's original recommendation for a pain consultation service was rejected, it was felt that there would be an advantage to having such a resource. The ideal, of course, would be to have a Hospice Unit within the hospital to show the staff "how to."

Dr. Heseltine presented the recommendations for management of chronic/terminal pain to the medical director, Dr. Sol Bernstein: (Appendix #5)

It has been established through evaluation of patient discharge plans and interviews with staff that the prescribing of narcotics for outpatients is significantly underused. We have found that very few medical residents or staff possess DEA (Drug Enforcement Administration) issued "triplicate" prescriptions. (Ed., California and nine other states require physicians to purchase special prescription forms for scheduled drugs such as opioids. One copy goes to the DEA; one to the pharmacy, and one remains with the physician.) The result is that patients with chronic pain that are maintained well on narcotics (in hospital) are often sent home on inadequate analgesia because no one is available to prescribe triplicate-required medication. As the problem is so widespread, and the need much greater than previously thought, the committee after considerable deliberation recommends that the Executive require all licensed physicians to possess DEA-issued triplicate prescriptions. By definition this would exclude interns but include faculty. The Committee believes that obtaining a license to practice medicine carries an ethical obligation that the physician be able to provide his/her patients with optimum pain management. A physician without "triplicates" is not in a position to do so. Physicians

3

that have no patient care responsibilities and insist on being exempt from this policy should be reviewed by an appropriate group.

The second recommendation by the committee is that a multi-disciplinary "pain management team" composed of interested physicians and other healthcare professionals be available for consultation by the medical and nursing staff. This team, in addition to ensuring appropriate management of difficult cases, would augment the teaching of pain management to the staff and improve the quality of patient care. Some of the members of the ad hoc committee would be willing to play a role in such a team.

A questionnaire survey of senior residents in Women's Hospital, regarding their ability to manage pain, revealed that 80% felt the need for more resident training in chronic pain management. A Women's Hospital nursing survey showed that 60% felt they needed additional information/education regarding pain management. (Appendix #6)

A patient audit by the Hospice Care/Pain Management Subcommittee reported the following major findings: (Appendix #7)

- Pain control was ineffective as only 23% of narcotic orders were for round- the-clock administration. Effectiveness was, for the most part, not charted.
- Psychosocial care mostly focused on placement though 73% of patients in the sample lived with primary care persons. Only four of 30 patients were referred for home care.
- Length of hospital stay averaged one month per patient.
- Reimbursement: 50% of the sample had no source of reimbursement.
- A comparison of home-care costs versus conventional hospital-care costs revealed that hospital-care costs were approximately $12 million per year for 500

terminally ill cancer patients. Home care would cost less than $1 million.

A repeat audit of general medicine and oncology wards reported by the Hospice Care/Pain Management Subcommittee in November 1986 included the following statement: (Appendix #8)

> In general, the audit demonstrated inappropriate ordering practices for pain control as well as lack of documentation regarding effectiveness or non-effectiveness of the pain medication. Out of the 16 patients sampled only one from a General Ward had a VNA (Visiting Nurse Association) referral. There were no VNA referrals from the Oncology/Hematology wards.

Follow the Money

The LAC-DHS Ad Hoc Committee on Hospice analyzed the financial feasibility of instituting a hospice program. (Appendix #1, page 14)

> Attempts by the Ad Hoc Committee to determine the financial feasibility of a County-operated hospice has brought mixed results. On the one hand, it is clear that the County could save money in the care of an individual dying patient by moving that patient to a less costly level of care. However, the Department of Health Services as a system would save money only if that now-empty acute care bed were not immediately refilled with other patients and if the necessary personnel and other supports were reduced accordingly.
>
> Since this is not likely to be the case, the only factor that would make it financially feasible to transfer the terminally ill patient to a hospice would be the existence of adequate reimbursement to meet the cost of hospice care. Unfortunately, at the present time,

the information with regards to the reimbursement for hospice care is too uncertain and too untested to allow for reliable financial predictions to be made with any degree of certainty.

In 1984, the LAC-DHS Ad Hoc Committee on Hospice did not even consider the additional Medi-Cal revenue loss from shifting substantial numbers of AIDS patients from hospitals to hospice programs. However, by the peak of the AIDS epidemic in 1994, LAC+USC Medical Center alone had an inpatient census of AIDS patients ranging from 80–100 per day, according to Fred Sattler, MD, chief of the AIDS Clinic. The census of LAC+USC Medical Center HIV/AIDS patients subsequently fell precipitously because of the advent of Medi-Cal and other funding for HIV/AIDS patients in the private sector. However, state-of-the-art palliative care and hospice for AIDS patients still would have further decreased LAC-DHS Medi-Cal reimbursement by tens of millions of dollars per year.

Launching of LAC+USC Medical Center Cancer and AIDS Pain Consultation Service

In a report to upper management regarding the findings of the Hospice Care/Pain Management Subcommittee, Dr. Sol Bernstein, LAC+USC Medical Director, wrote the understatement, "In summary, we have confirmed that pain management may in fact be less than optimal in many patients treated as inpatients." (Appendix #2) Dr. Bernstein relayed the results of the LAC+USC Medical Center Hospice Subcommittee audit and re-audit of pain management to LAC-DHS administration and mentioned that a Cancer Pain Consultation Service was beginning under my direction. (Appendix #9)

Chapter 2

The Cancer and AIDS Pain Service
1987–1992

In February 1987, my seven-year campaign to begin a Cancer and AIDS Pain Service in the Los Angeles County-Department of Health (LAC-DHS) was finally realized. Based on the recommendation of the Hospice Care/Pain Management Subcommittee, the Cancer and AIDS Pain Service began with a research/clinical nurse and one physician— me. (Appendix #10) The only cost to the hospital of this new consultation service was the loss of my time in general internal medicine. From the pharmaceutical company, Purdue Frederick, I negotiated funding for a research study of long-acting morphine. This money paid for the pain management nurse on the Service.

The volume of consults quickly grew to make it one of the ten busiest palliative care services in the United States. In 1991 and 1992, I sought to significantly increase the resources allocated to palliative care by campaigning for an inpatient palliative care unit. (Appendices #11, #12, #13, #14, #15, #16, #17, #18, #19, #20, #21, #22, #23, #24, #25, #26) Jonathan Weisbuch, MD, medical director of the LAC-DHS, actively helped in this effort in many ways, including arranging for me to meet with T. George Wilson, MD, Chief, Medi-Cal Policy Section in Sacramento, and his staff.

I explained to the Medi-Cal Policy personnel that I was a consultant to other physicians at the hospital in the management of their patients' pain from cancer and AIDS. A nurse worked with me to help control that pain. Our care for terminally ill patients was rooted in the hospice philosophy and employed hospice techniques. When no cure of these patients is possible, the hospice approach emphasizes the management of pain and the provision of psychological, social, and spiritual support for both patients and family members. Using a team approach, we often called in physical therapists, psychiatrists, anesthesiologists, and other specialists.

To describe the situation in terms of human suffering and wasted resources, I related the state of palliative care at the LAC+USC

Medical Center to Dr. Wilson and his staff with the following example of a patient referred to the Cancer and AIDS Pain Service:

> Mr. Lee (not his real name) was a 52-year-old Korean man who had undergone surgery for stomach cancer 13 months earlier in Seoul, Korea. Since the cancer had already spread to the liver and elsewhere, he had received intra-operative chemotherapy followed by conventional outpatient chemotherapy. When this failed, he immigrated to Los Angeles hoping for a cure.

> At my hospital, he received an experimental chemotherapy drug for six months. This also failed to control his disease. It lowered his blood platelet count, thus increasing his chances of bleeding from the remaining abdominal tumors. As an outpatient, multiple transfusions of blood were given because of hemorrhage through the gastrointestinal tract.

> One bleeding episode required hospitalization to achieve control. During that time, after discussing it with his doctor, Mr. Lee agreed to a "do-not-resuscitate" order that was then recorded in his chart. Unfortunately, on discharge from hospital he was not referred to our visiting nurse association hospice program or to my Cancer and AIDS Pain Service.

> He had been out of the hospital only three weeks when he began to vomit blood and was again rushed to our emergency room. He was immediately transfused with blood and quickly moved to our new, ultramodern intensive care unit. When bleeding persisted, he underwent angiography (i.e., an X-ray dye study) of his abdominal blood vessels and the bleeding artery was blocked off by an injection of a special material. Soon the specialists in interventional radiology repeated this procedure because of recurrent bleeding. Because the cancer was so advanced and the patient's inability to take food while the acute bleeding problem

persisted, the intensive care unit physicians ordered total parenteral (intravenous) nutrition to prevent malnourishment. This provided about 3,000 calories per day, along with plenty of intravenous fluid.

After more time in the intensive care unit, Mr. Lee developed a fever; his doctors promptly ordered antibiotics. Later, when the fever persisted and blood cultures showed infection with resistant bacteria, he was switched to more powerful antibiotics.

On the tenth hospital day, a new intensive care unit doctor discussed with Mr. Lee and his family the seriousness of his condition. Mr. Lee again requested not to be resuscitated if his heart stopped beating. The doctor dutifully noted this in the chart. However, Mr. Lee remained in the ICU.

Abdominal pain had been a big problem even before this hospitalization. At least six months before hospitalization, Mr. Lee's oncologist had prescribed prolonged-release morphine. While in intensive care, the pain increased despite institution of intravenous morphine infusion and titrating the dose to 20 milligrams per hour (a high dose).

Mr. Lee's doctor asked the anesthesiology pain service to administer a nerve block to better control his severe pain. After deliberation for several days, the anesthesiologists declined to carry out the nerve block procedure for fear of causing internal bleeding, and possibly shortening his life.

At his wit's end, on the 21st day in the intensive care unit, Mr. Lee's intern called on me to offer new suggestions for the management of Mr. Lee's pain. He had observed that a marked accumulation of fluid in Mr. Lee's abdomen was now also contributing to the pain.

The intern told me that because of Mr. Lee's pain and the overall poor prognosis, Mr. Lee had been begging for a lethal overdose of medication—in essence, begging for euthanasia. The young doctor was obviously in an uncomfortable position, as any doctor would be.

This case offered me an excellent opportunity to teach the intern some of the basics of palliative care. I explained that with a terminally ill patient in this situation, although we cannot honor a request for euthanasia, physicians are under no legal, moral, or other obligation to continue therapies designed to prolong life, such as blood product transfusions, total parenteral nutrition, and antibiotics.

I suggested that a paracentesis (removal of abdominal fluid) be done to decrease the pressure in Mr. Lee's abdomen. I also requested that the intravenous fluids, including the total parenteral nutrition, be stopped in order to prevent further misery from the IV fluid accumulating in the abdominal cavity. Finally, I recommended an increase in the morphine infusion dose to 30 milligrams per hour.

The next day when I saw Mr. Lee, he had been transferred to a "closely monitored area" on a regular medical ward. He was in coma and the morphine infusion had been stopped. Very distraught relatives filed in and out of his room for short visits, making their way between the hospital staff and the life-support technology.

Skimming the chart (three thick volumes had accumulated during the 22-day ICU stay), I noted that the paracentesis had not been done, again for fear of causing bleeding and the shortening of Mr. Lee's life. Two expensive intravenous antibiotics, total parenteral nutrition feedings, and frequent insulin injections had continued. Blood cultures drawn two or three days earlier showed that two types of bacteria were growing despite the antibiotics. Other laboratory tests continued to be ordered.

I spoke at length with the new intern and resident about what to do if abdominal or other pain reemerged and, in general, concerning palliative care in this type of situation. During the following night, Mr. Lee woke up enough to express pain. More morphine was given intravenously, but initially did not work. Instead of giving Mr. Lee higher doses of morphine, the doctors had injected Valium, which only quieted him down.

In the morning, the staff had suddenly become concerned with inappropriate utilization of the hospital's resources (the closely monitored unit) and ordered Mr. Lee's transfer to the regular ward. The total parenteral nutrition, antibiotics, and insulin could all be continued on the regular ward, but the morphine infusion pump could not.

The new intern wrote an order for prolonged release morphine sulfate to be crushed and given through the gastric feeding tube. I pointed out to the staff the problems with this strategy. Crushing prolonged-release morphine converts it into immediate-release morphine, which lasts only about four hours. In an acutely ill person with sepsis, widespread cancer, tense fluid throughout his abdomen, and low blood pressure, oral analgesics or other medications would not be reliably absorbed from the gastrointestinal tract. The nursing administration made an exception and allowed the morphine pump for his final hours. The pump was not turned on since he never came out of coma.

I wish there were a happy ending to this story, but there is not. When Mr. Lee died, the doctors told the family that they had done all that could be done medically to save him. No one could be charged with malpractice for undertreating pain, since this is not unusual care of the dying in America. However, a lack of training in palliative care and the obstacles built into our medical care system had prevented even rudimentary pain and symptom control measures for Mr. Lee, let alone help with the psychological and emotional process of preparing for his death.

In a time of dire shortages of health care funding for the poor, this hospitalization cost the taxpayer over $50,000 (1991 dollars). This hospitalization served only to magnify pain and suffering enough for him to beg for euthanasia. For Mr. Lee, euthanasia was not the answer. Physician training in palliative care offers the prospect of a far better solution.[1]

This story led to more recognition of the cost of futile care in the state Medi-Cal administration and an assurance of reimbursement policies that would not penalize the County for establishing an acute-level palliative care unit. In a letter to Dr. Weisbuch dated December 10, 1992, Sally Lee, Chief of Medi-Cal Operations Division, said: (Appendix #27)

While the Medi-Cal Program can only reimburse for medically necessary services, specific approval by the Medi-Cal Program is not required in order to establish these services at LAC-USC Medical Center or other Los Angeles County Hospitals. Determination of specific wards, staffing ratios, and professional services are matters of County administration under hospital licensure and certification requirements. Medi-Cal's primary concern is that Medi-Cal beneficiaries treated in such a unit require and receive only medically necessary, acute level services under any acute inpatient settings.

The subject proactive approach in identifying areas where significant cost saving can be achieved by both the County and the Medi-Cal Program is commended. However, the overall success of this proposal, in terms of cost savings and quality of care, will largely depend on the County's ability to establish the services that will be required beyond acute hospitalization. These would include the transition to traditional hospice as well as the availability of home health services. The County may want to consider the feasibility of becoming a separate provider for these services. This would allow the County greater flexibility in managing these cases without having to depend on other providers.

Unfortunately, the LAC-DHS did not act on Dr. Weisbuch's recommendation and the encouragement by the Medi-Cal Program administrators to initiate an acute level palliative care unit. Not long after these events, LAC-DHS Director Robert Gates fired Dr. Weisbuch as LAC-DHS Medical Director, possibly, in part, because of his advocacy of more LAC-DHS resources devoted to the care of the dying.

Chapter 3

Conflicts over Resources for Palliative Care

In September 1992, Dr. David Goldstein, my supervisor, gave me two new assignments. I was to supervise two physician assistants on an inpatient ward service (Appendix #28) and also to lead an admitting internal medicine ward team for the month of November 1992. My previously assigned other duty was to supervise about 10 residents one-half day per week in a general internal medicine clinic. I protested verbally and in writing with a formal grievance (Appendix #29), but I could not convince my supervisor that doing these two new jobs along with the Cancer and AIDS Pain Service was physically impossible. I couldn't physically comply with Dr. Goldstein's order to supervise the physician assistants from 8 AM to 4 PM Monday through Friday while also consulting on the Cancer and AIDS Pain Service. Nurses who worked with hospice patients wrote letters on my behalf. (Appendix #30, #31, #32)

David Hancock, a non-physician LAC+USC Medical Center administrator, served as arbitrator for the third and final level grievance hearing of my work assignment change. He filed a detailed report to Jerry Buckingham, LAC+USC Medical Center Executive Director. The report was favorable to me but deferred to LAC+USC Medical Director Dr. Sol Bernstein. (Appendices #33, #34) Dr. Bernstein agreed with me that the assignment was impossible. He deleted Dr. Goldstein's harassing letters charging insubordination from my personnel file. (Appendices #35, #36, #37, #38) Although I filed an official grievance, Dr. Bernstein treated the matter informally and refused to document the resolution of the conflict in writing despite my written requests that he fulfill his obligation and do so. In a memo to Dr. Bernstein dated December 29, 1992, I finally documented the resolution of the grievance. (Appendix #39)

Losing this dispute made Dr. Goldstein even angrier. In a memo dated January 12, 1993, he continued my assignment on the Cancer and AIDS Pain Service 12 months per year but added four months of supervising internal medicine ward admitting teams. I still supervised a one-half day per week outpatient internal medicine clinic. Out of spite, he again gave me an impossible work situation stating: (Appendix #40)

> Your work hours per week are 40, starting at 8:00 AM to 4:30 PM which includes a half hour lunch but does not include two fifteen minute breaks in the eight-hour day. . . . Any overtime request must have my prior approval.

He anticipated that newly instituted rules from Dr. Bernstein regarding overtime (Appendix #41), apparently with me in mind, would cover this new strategy. As the only physician on the Cancer and AIDS Pain Service that now had about 20 new consults per month and over 100 home patients being monitored at any given time, I could not limit my hours to 8 AM to 4:30 PM, Monday to Friday. Besides attempting to put me in my place after his loss of face due to the previous grievance outcome, this appeared to be an attempt to confiscate my overtime hours, which until then averaged 15–20 per week.

This policy discriminated against me as a County-employed physician versus the USC-employed physicians that Dr. Goldstein also supervised without imposing this kind of rigid schedule. Another new rule regarding overtime that greatly affected my situation was that "overtime may be accrued only for work performed on Medical Center grounds and for County-related duties." (Appendix #41) Since I was on call 24 hours per day, seven days per week, I spent many hours per week away from the hospital speaking on the phone with interns, residents, nurses, and patients, phoning in orders, and otherwise dealing with the problems of my patients.

I asked for a clarification of this new directive and requested to average 40 hours per week on a flexible schedule. (Appendix #42) Dr. Goldstein denied my request with memos that hardened his position. (Appendices #43, #44) For instance, I had a speaking engagement on a weekday morning and asked for prior authorization to work 12 PM to 8 PM. Dr. Goldstein approved my absence from 8 AM to 12 PM but disallowed my "overtime" from 4:30 PM to 8 PM on the same day. (Appendix #45) He refused to answer another letter requesting clarification of the overtime rules. (Appendices #46, #47)

16

After I filed another grievance, Dr. Bernstein again called an "informal meeting" to resolve this matter and other conflicts. He used the word "chickenshit" to describe the aspect of Dr. Goldstein's directive that I work only 8 AM to 4:30 PM Monday through Friday. However, we could not resolve the other scheduling issues, and Dr. Bernstein again refused to document in writing the results of the meeting.

I summarized the meeting content in a memo to Dr. Bernstein dated February 26, 1993 (Appendix #48), and followed up with related correspondence. (Appendices #49, #50)

In the hearing on this matter, I argued, "Dr. David Goldstein ordered unfair and prejudiced limitations on my work schedule (memo January 12, 1993). This denies reimbursement for some of my County time performing the duties in my job description. Other physicians in the General Internal Medicine (GIM) section do not have these scheduling restrictions." An excerpt of this grievance follows:

> This grievance derives from a fundamental conflict of interest which exists with Dr. Goldstein's role as supervisor of GIM physicians, some engaged solely in LAC-USC duties and others dividing their time between USC private practice and research. Since Dr. Goldstein's supervisors direct him to build the private practice and research components of the section, he is under pressure to sacrifice LAC-USC teaching and clinical care. In effect, the above mentioned work schedule memo requires me to choose between drastically reducing clinical services to LAC-USC patients and working many unreimbursed overtime hours. (Appendix #51)

In that year I gave 30–40 lectures to physicians in other hospitals, many out of town, so the lack of a flexible schedule, including recognition of out-of-hospital work on my timecard, meant an incredible number of uncompensated hours worked. (Appendix #52) On April 19, 1993, Dr. Bernstein finally denied my grievance without addressing my charge of conflict of interest. (Appendix #53)

My unsuccessful letter of appeal to Robert Gates, Director of the LAC-DHS, contained the following paragraph:

I complain about this situation because it is part of a pattern of using LA County resources (in this case my professional services) for the financial benefit of USC University Hospital. I work under administrators whose top priorities are the success of the USC hospital, the USC private practice program, and fundable research studies. Dr. Goldstein's transparent scheme to confiscate a portion of my livelihood is supported by upper level USC administrators all of whom have a conflict of interest in dealing with LAC physician employees. (Appendix #54)

Mr. Gates sided with the hospital's management. (Appendix #55)

As an unintended benefit to me arising out of this battle, Dr. Goldstein assigned me to supervise medical residents in evaluating and treating patients referred to the Cancer and AIDS Pain Service. (Appendix #56) Perhaps he hoped to make me redundant by having the medical residents do my work. I proposed some variations on Dr. Goldstein's protocol to prevent delays in treating pain due to the busy schedules of the residents. (Appendix #57) He insisted that consults be called to the internal medicine office, rather than directly to me, but allowed for me to be paged if the delay would be more than two hours. (Appendix #58) Dr. Goldstein also forbade the residents to manage outpatients. (Appendix #59) Handling outpatient problems is an essential component to teaching doctors about palliative care.

Despite these difficulties, supervising two medical residents per month and seeing the inpatient consults was a mutually satisfactory arrangement. Teaching these residents the art and practical details of caring for the dying gave me great satisfaction. It did not reduce my workload, however. The enhanced exposure and popularity of the Service, in part due to the rotating residents, caused the average number of monthly consults to rise from about 20 to 35. Almost all cases still required my direct and ongoing involvement, since I still had to write over 90% of the opioid medication prescriptions. Despite the hospital administration's "carry your triplicates" mandate resulting from the Hospice Care/Pain Management Subcommittee, few residents or attendings had or carried the required triplicate prescription forms.

18

In June 1993, Dr. Goldstein assigned me to supervise an internal medicine admitting team ward in addition to my regular duties of supervising the one-half day per week internal medicine clinic, and also attending on the Cancer and AIDS Pain Service. Unlike the previous months in which I had additional attending duties (Appendix #60), Dr. Goldstein refused to approve the 15–20 overtime hours that it took me to accomplish all my tasks. (Appendix #61)

I filed a grievance (Appendix #62) that was granted by Dr. Bernstein but, pointedly, only for that particular month. (Appendix #63) For the next few months, Dr. Goldstein approved my overtime when I did the extra ward attending duties. (Appendices #64, #65)

A Vacation to Remember

I had been pre-approved to take my vacation in July 1993. However, Dr. Goldstein had forgotten that he signed my vacation authorization, and his office staff misplaced his copy of the form. On July 8, 1993, he sent the following memo to the LAC+USC Medical Center internal medicine personnel officer with a copy to me: (Appendix #66)

> It is my understanding that Dr. Cundiff has taken a vacation. No request for this vacation was received in my office, and I am writing this letter to protest this unacceptable behavior.

After I produced my copy of the vacation request form signed by Dr. Goldstein, he still refused to apologize verbally or in writing. Consequently, I referred the matter to Dr. Goldstein's boss, Richard Tannen, MD, Chief of Internal Medicine. The following was Dr. Tannen's response to my letter: (Appendix #67)

> Thank you for your memorandum of July 27, 1993 regarding your recent vacation. I did look into the matter and found that there was some confusion about your vacation approval.
>
> Once Mr. Navarro reviewed the records and informed Dr. Goldstein that your time had been approved, the

19

matter was closed. I have been informed that Dr. Goldstein's memo to Mr. Navarro about your vacation has not been placed in your personnel file. All of us regret any inconvenience this may have caused you.

Overtime Denial Grievance

On January 6, 1994, Dr. Goldstein issued an order that required the LA County-paid physicians in General Internal Medicine—but not the USC-paid physicians—to sign-in and sign-out each day. (Appendix #68) I stated my objections to Dr. Goldstein, Dr. Bernstein, and to Robert Gates, claiming that this represented discrimination against LA County-paid physicians. (Appendices #69, #70, #71) Dr. Goldstein did not consider the directive discriminatory (Appendix #72). Ed Martinez, the new Executive Director of the LAC+USC Medical Center, and proxy for Mr. Gates, sided with Dr. Goldstein while steadfastly refusing to address the discrimination issue. (Appendices #73, #74, #75, #76)

Dr. Goldstein's office staff analyzed the sign-in/sign-out sheets and reported that I averaged about 11 hours per day, whether I had additional ward attending duties or not. (Appendix #77) My weekends attending on the wards and hours of calls from home were not included in the analysis, however. Mysteriously, based on this audit of my work hours, he justified a policy of permitting only one extra hour per weekday worked when I was assigned to additional ward supervision duties.

I wrote Dr. Bernstein to update him on this issue on March 27, 1994 (Appendix #78) and met with him about this and other matters on May 5, 1994. (Appendix #79) However, management continued to stonewall. (Appendices #80, #81, #82) Dr. Goldstein proceeded to deny all my weekday overtime (Appendix #83) and alter the hours on my timecard. (Appendices #84, #85) Administration gave me an ultimatum to sign my timecard with the false low hours. (Appendix #86) My appeal to Dr. Bernstein, who was close to retirement, fell on deaf ears. (Appendix #87)

In September 1994, Dr. Goldstein again assigned me to attend on medical inpatient wards in addition to staffing the Cancer and AIDS Pain Service and a one-half day per week internal medicine clinic. I submitted pre-approval forms for 15–20 hours per week of overtime as this assignment had previously required. (Appendices #88, #89) Again, Dr. Goldstein would not approve the necessary overtime. (Appendix #90) I submit that no physician anywhere has managed this clinical load in 40 hours per week. The statement of my grievance on this matter went as follows: (Appendix #91)

> This is a repeat of a grievance regarding denial of overtime for June 1993. That grievance was also heard by Ms. Hernandez and resolved in my favor August 20, 1993 by Dr. Sol Bernstein.

> In the current grievance I specify September 1994 and all other months in which I am assigned medical ward attending duties in addition to my usual assignment of directing the Cancer and AIDS Pain Service, as well as supervising a medical clinic.

> In September 1994, the Cancer and AIDS Pain Service had 55 new consults (an eight-year record) and followed over 200 active patients. In addition, I was responsible for over 120 hospitalized patients as medical ward attending.

Dr. Ronald Kaufman, the new LAC+USC Medical Center medical director, denied this grievance based on the time sheet data that I averaged about 55 hours at the hospital per week whether I attended on medical inpatient wards or not. (Appendix #92) This did not consider the many hours at home that I spent on the phone dealing with Cancer and AIDS Pain Service and inpatient medicine problems.

Medical Disability

While fighting these battles about overtime and having to clock in and out, I developed weight-bearing pain in my left hip. I consulted (John) Chang-Zern Hong, MD, an associate professor of physical medicine and rehabilitation from UC Irvine School of Medicine. On April 23, 1994, he wrote on my behalf to Dr. Richard Tannen, Chief of Internal Medicine, saying: (Appendix #93)

Dr. David Cundiff is under my care for the treatment
of sprain of left hip with subtrochanteric bursitis and
tendentious. He also has myofascial pain in the left
gluteal muscles, pyriformis, and iliopsosas. Over the
past six-months, he had three relapses of this
condition which required him to walk with crutches.
Most recently, he has been on crutches for the past
two weeks. I injected the left hip bursa with Decadron
LA today so, hopefully, this will speed his recovery.
However, until the acute inflammation resolves, he
must avoid weight bearing on the left leg.

Due to the current acute inflammation episode and the
relapsing nature of Dr. Cundiff's condition, I am
advising him not to take on the extra duties of ward
medicine attending in May 1994. The stress of him
working above 40 hours per week would likely
aggravate his tendonitis.

On May 1, 1994, Dr. Goldstein responded with the following
memo: (Appendix #94)

I have read the letter from Dr. Hong and appreciate
its contents. You have been assigned to work the
Medicine Ward Attending in May 1994. Therefore, you
will work your 40 hours as supervisor for the
housestaff on your assigned team. Any hours in excess
of your regular 40 hours that may be required for the
Cancer Pain Management Service is to be handled by
either the GIM (General Internal Medicine) medicine
residents of the month or your nurse, Cadena Bedney.

I responded with the following memo on May 2, 1994: (Appendix
#95)

I received your letter responding to my physician
restricting me to 40 hours hospital work per week due
to my left hip bursitis. The Cancer and AIDS Pain
Service now follows about 250 active patients, 95% of

22

whom are at home or in nursing homes. We have been averaging about 40 new consults per month in recent months. The medical residents rotating on the service see only the inpatients. As a nurse, Cadena Bedney cannot make medical decisions or prescribe medication, which is required to run the Cancer and AIDS Pain Service. If I attend on the Medical Service, I cannot avoid working 55 to 60 hour weeks. Additional physician staffing for the Service would be needed to reduce my hours of work.

Because of the realities of the Cancer and AIDS Pain Service workload and my medical condition, I will accept the medical ward attending assignment under protest.

Dr. Bernstein didn't respond to my appeal (Appendix #96) and Robert Gates' assistant denied it. (Appendices #97, #98) Gloria Molina, member of the LA County Board of Supervisors, also concurred. (Appendices #99, #100) My remission due to the steroid injection of my weight bearing pain lasted until the end of May 1994. Then I again had to return to crutch walking due to hip pain.

It became increasingly clear that my toxic work environment related directly to the dysfunctional Medicaid funding system for indigent patient care. Inpatient care was a cash cow, while outpatient care like hospice lost money.

The Angel of Death Case

Newspapers, television, and radio sensationalized the case of a hospice nurse, Darlene Leon, RN, who was accused of euthanizing 18 of her patients. Because the case threatened the credibility of the entire hospice establishment, I spent a week of my own time gathering the facts of the case from the San Bernardino Sheriff's Department and critically analyzing the information. I sent the resulting article (Appendix #237) to the San Bernardino Sheriff who immediately dropped the case. Remarkably, the media rapidly lost interest in the case because of the innocence of the accused. The media chose not to use the occasion to educate the public about hospice.

Trying to Institutionalize the Cancer and AIDS Pain Service

On November 30, 1993, I sent Dr. Goldstein a memorandum requesting permission for an unpaid leave of absence during the year 1995. I did this partly because I was co-authoring with Mary Ellen McCarthy, Ph.D., a book on health care reform: *The Right Medicine— How To Make Health Care Reform Work Today.*[2] I also wanted to encourage the LAC+USC Medical Center administration to institutionalize the Cancer and AIDS Pain Service. I asked if he would assign no less than three internal medicine attending physicians to do rounds with the Cancer and AIDS Pain Service and become familiar with palliative care and the treatment of pain. (Appendix #101) Dr. Goldstein approved my one-year leave of absence on February 4, 1994, but declined to provide physician coverage for the Cancer and AIDS Pain Service while I was away. (Appendix #102) My appeals to Dr. Bernstein on February 24, 1994 (Appendix #103) and the new medical director of LAC+USC Medical Center, Dr. Ronald Kaufman, on August 29, 1994 (Appendix #104) to "institutionalize" the Cancer and AIDS Pain Service by assigning new staff went unanswered.

Hundreds of doctors and nurses and other hospital staff signed a petition requesting the continuation of the Cancer and AIDS Pain Service. (Appendix #105) Some patients wrote letters to administrators. (Appendices #106, #107, #108) Finally, on October 24, 1994, administration relented and appointed Dr. Leslie Blackhall as Acting Director of the Pain and Palliative Care Service (a new name) effective January 1, 1995. (Appendix #109) Dr. Goldstein rejected my suggestion that she begin immediately to become oriented to the new duties.

Medical Leave of Absence

My left hip pain and requirement for crutch walking increased during and after the grueling month of September 1994 due to the additional attending duties and a record number of Cancer and AIDS Pain Service consults (55). My physical medicine and rehabilitation physician, Dr. Hong, recommended that I be excused from attending on inpatient medicine wards in November 1994. (Appendix #110) Dr.

24

Goldstein's response dated October 20, 1994 was as follows: (Appendix #111)

> I have received a copy of a letter from Dr. Chang-Zern Hong, which was addressed to Dr. Tannen and dated October 4, 1994. Dr. Hong recommends that you be excused from the ward attending duties. If in the opinion of your physician you can come to work, then I must insist that you comply with your assigned duties as ward attending for the month of November.
>
> I sympathize with your reoccurrence of the bursitis, but this should not be due to <u>increased activity</u>. While you are attending on Medicine, the Cancer and AIDS Pain Service can be handled by your nurse, Cadena Bedney, along with the help of the Residents on the Consult Service and the Anesthesia Service.
>
> If you come to work in November and do not report as assigned to your Ward Attending responsibility, then I will unfortunately deem you insubordinate.

Subsequently, Dr. Hong put me on two months medical leave beginning October 29, 1994. (Appendix #112)

No physician was assigned to the Pain and Palliative Care Service, and I was continually called at home for consults and problems. My phone record showed up to 80 calls per day of Pain and Palliative Care Service business for which I was not compensated since I was on medical leave. Thankfully, I could do the work lying down rather than sitting, standing, or walking. My appeal to Dr. Kaufman for a 40 hour work week went unanswered. (Appendix #113) I also filed a complaint with the Equal Employment Opportunity Commission during my medical leave. (Appendices #114, #115) Because of a large backlog of cases, this was not addressed for more than one year and then found not to fall within their guidelines. (Appendices #116, #117, #118, #119, #120, #121) I didn't have the money or the time to appeal this decision to superior court.

Because of my new medical problem, and the fact that my recently published book did not have the impact I had hoped for, I decided against taking the unpaid sabbatical to promote my ideas on health care reform. Dr. Hong extended my disability leave until mid-January 1995 (Appendices #122) when I joined Dr. Blackhall and the Service.

Written Warning/ Future Activities

In memorandums dated January 25, 1995, January 31, 1995, and February 2, 1995, from Dr. Goldstein to me, he described his poor impression of my ability to administer the Pain and Palliative Care Service. (Appendices #123, #124, #125) He cited my provision of primary services instead of a consultative service and complained that I treated patients directly without teaching the housestaff, faculty, and nurses about how to manage patients with chronic pain. He stated that by my taking over the pain treatment of patients, I caused internal medicine graduating physicians to be lacking in chronic pain management experience and skills. Dr. Goldstein faulted my attempts to integrate other disciplines such as Oncology, Anesthesia, Neurology and Psychiatry into the activities of the Cancer and AIDS Pain Service. For these reasons he fired me as director of the Pain and Palliative Care Service and promoted Dr. Blackhall to the director position permanently.

My response in the form of a grievance maintained that this highly subjective impression of Dr. Goldstein related more to his personal vendetta against me than to my performance as director of the Pain and Palliative Care Service. (Appendices #126) Regarding my provision of primary care services for patients on whom we were called to consult, I did not tell patients not to go to their oncology, hematology, or AIDS doctors. I only offered to be the backup person to call if their regular doctors were not controlling pain.

Many patients with end-stage diseases admitted to the hospital with pain and/or out-of-control symptoms required a home or nursing home hospice referral. The physician of record for the patients needed to be knowledgeable in pain treatment and palliative care and available 24 hours per day, seven days per week. The fellows in medical oncology and hematology and the primary care providers for AIDS patients were neither trained in palliative care nor available at all times. The new oncology fellows, who began working in July, frequently did not get their triplicates for narcotics prescriptions until

September or later. To provide the optimum palliative care with the resources available, I became the physician-of-record for terminally ill patients by default.

Successful long-term management of chronic pain from cancer and AIDS was largely an outpatient enterprise, although the initial consultation usually occurred in the inpatient setting. The oncology fellows and AIDS primary care providers were kept too busy with managing their in-hospital duties to closely monitor their out-of-hospital patients. For many patients the primary care resident physicians had been unable to effectively treat pain because of lack of triplicates, time pressures, dysfunctional attitudes about treating chronic pain patients with opioids, knowledge deficits concerning palliative care, or other reasons.

No palliative care specialist could effectively supervise 100–200 residents and fellows simultaneously in the treatment of pain and other symptoms of 200+ inpatients and outpatients with advanced diseases. Most of these physicians-in-training did not have their triplicate prescription forms and their faculty attendings were often inaccessible, so they couldn't directly provide pain treatment for their patients anyway.

However, I had no interest in cornering the knowledge concerning pain control and palliative care at the LAC+USC Medical Center. During the tenure of the Cancer and AIDS Pain Service and the Pain and Palliative Care Service from February 1987 to September 1995, I welcomed any and all students, residents, and fellows to rotate on the Service. Takers included six psychiatry residents, two medical students, one anesthesia resident, one hematology fellow, one medical oncology fellow, and about 50 medical residents doing one-month rotations. Residents gave the Cancer and AIDS Pain Service rotation high praise for teaching. (Appendix #127) My internal medicine teaching evaluations by the residents were also consistently above average. (Appendices #128, #129)

Although the substance of Dr. Goldstein's criticisms of me was political rather than documented performance deficits, his memo to me went into my personnel file and became one of the charges supporting my termination from the County.

Disregarding a Direct Order

On January 25, 1995 when he fired me as director of the Pain and Palliative Care Service, Dr. Goldstein told me to refer all calls requesting consultations to the internal medicine secretary during normal working hours and to the on-call medical resident of the day for after hours referrals. (Appendix #124) I filed a grievance (Appendix #131) and protested to Dr. Goldstein's boss, Richard Tannen, MD, Chief of Internal Medicine, that this would inevitably delay the treatment of patients in severe pain. (Appendix #132) I requested Dr. Tannen's urgent attention since this was a patient care issue. Dr. Tannen never replied. On February 9, 1995, Dr. Goldstein sent me a memorandum entitled: "Written warning – Disregarding a Direct Order to Change Phone message for Pain & Palliative Care Service." (Appendix #130)

Dr. Goldstein had signs posted to implement his order (Appendix #133), but the nurses and residents often persisted and called me directly. After I received Dr. Goldstein's reprimand, I changed the outgoing message on my answer machine, but direct requests to me for assistance with treating patients with pain continued.

In subsequent years, the Anesthesia Department ran LAC+USC Pain Service, and the method of calling consults evolved back to paging the consultant directly because of the problems of unnecessary delays. (Appendices #134, #135)

"Insubordination" Regarding My Physical Disability

On my return to work on January 15, 1995, I still required crutches to walk. Dr. Goldstein asked me to attend on a medicine ward service in March, May, September, and November. (Appendix #136) I sent a responding memorandum dated February 5, 1995, saying that my doctor advised me not to attempt ward attending until I could walk without crutches for several months. (Appendix #137) Dr. Hong also sent Dr. Goldstein a letter dated February 7, 1995 stating, "I have advised him to return to work with the same restrictions as mentioned previously, including use of crutches for walking longer than 30 yards and frequent rest as needed, for at least

28

two months." (Appendix #138) My memorandum to Dr. Goldstein, dated February 24, 1995, said the following: (Appendix #139)

> My left hip bursitis is still symptomatic requiring crutch walking two weeks after the last Decadron injection. Minimizing weight bearing remains the only effective treatment. My physician, Dr. John Hong, advises me not to do medical ward attending until the bursitis has significantly improved. He does not want me ward attending in March and May of this year.

On February 27, 1995, Dr. Goldstein responded with the following memorandum entitled: "Attending/Rounding on Ward." (Appendix #141)

> I am in receipt of your memorandum dated February 24, 1995. Your desire to avoid your duties as supervisor and instructor of Housestaff inpatient rounds is inappropriate.
>
> As we have discussed previously and I have written previously, your job duties are no more onerous than other faculty (please see copies of memos dated 1/12/93, 10/20/94, and your 1/20/95 Attending Staff Evaluation). (Appendices #41, #111, and #140) You cannot act as your own agent, deciding what you do and what you don't wish to do. Your physician's recommendations do not limit you from coming to work, and while you are at work I will decide what you do. You presently are going to other wards to see consults, and I have even seen you walk across the street to the USC Campus.
>
> Based on the above comments, I have judged you insubordinate and may take necessary disciplinary actions such as suspension and/or possible discharge.

29

A copy of this memorandum will be placed in your
official Personnel file and will become a part of your
permanent file.

It was true that my job duties were no more onerous than other
USC faculty members in General Internal Medicine. However, the
average attending physician in my department worked 60–80 hours
per week. Because of this physical disability I could not maintain my
previous frenetic pace of work. However, I could work 40 hours per
week, which was the requirement for my job. In 40 hours per week, no
one could supervise the residents on the Pain and Palliative Care
Service as well as lead residents and students on an inpatient ward
service. Residents throughout the Medical Center referred 35 new
consults per month on average to the Pain and Palliative Care Service
and we also followed 200+ active patients at home or in nursing
homes.

My additional duties included supervising four residents and
students on an inpatient ward service with 100–120 acute care
admissions per month and teaching and monitoring 10 additional
residents in a one-half-day per week internal medicine ambulatory
care clinic. Under protest, I did attend on the medicine service in
addition to my other responsibilities in March 1995 and May 1995.
(Appendix #142) However, this insubordination charge remained as
one of the grounds for my removal from County service. (Appendix
#230)

To add to the work of the Pain and Palliative Care Service, the
Anesthesia Pain Service closed March 16, 1995. (Appendix #143) The
Anesthesia Pain Service focused primarily on nerve blocks and
epidural infusions of opioids. They were not interested in prescribing
opioids or other medications. However, it was useful to have their help
with some patients with difficult to manage pain.

By July 1995, I again required a medical leave from work due to
the exacerbation of left hip pain by constant weight bearing. During
this two-month disability leave of absence, I began to receive a series
of injections of inflammatory substances into my low back and
sacroiliac joints called prolotherapy (also termed proliferative
therapy, sclerotherapy, or reconstructive joint therapy) under Dr.
Bjorn Eek, an orthopedic surgeon. This treatment worked very well

and enabled me to return to work without crutches in September 1995.

My symptoms continued to improve until February 1996. However, more severe pain returned accompanied by urogenital symptoms suggesting nerve entrapment in my sacral plexus. Further diagnostic evaluation in May 1996 revealed the real cause of my hip pain to be narrowing of part of my spine causing pinching of nerves (i.e., severe bilateral lateral foraminal stenosis at my fifth lumbar–first sacral vertebral levels). Gradually, my pain and disability became unbearable, and I underwent laminectomy with fusion of these two vertebras on June 21, 1996. (Appendix #144) This finally relieved the nerve entrapment symptoms. I continued with frequent flare-ups of back pain but much less severe than before the surgery.

It turned out that the degeneration of my fifth lumbar–first sacral vertebral bones was caused by wearing a 1/2" lift in my left shoe because of a leg length difference. The lift was prescribed by a chiropractor and subsequently approved by several physicians. Removing the lift, performing therapeutic exercises, and receiving further prolotherapy injections considerably improved the situation.

Chapter 4

LAC-DHS Financial Crisis in 1995

A financial crisis gripped the Los Angeles County-Department of Health Services (LAC-DHS) and all of Los Angeles County government in the recession years of the early 1990s. Facing possible bankruptcy of the entire LA County government, Sally Reed, LA County CEO, recommended that the LA County Board of Directors close my hospital, the LAC-USC Medical Center.

The impoverished East LA barrios let out an immediate and forceful outcry. Due to increasing political pressure, just before the 1994 elections, President Clinton approved a federal bailout of the LAC-DHS that eventually totaled over $1.2 billion. Hoping to prod the LAC-DHS into needed reforms in keeping with the cost effectiveness of managed care, President Clinton attached strings to the money that would force a major shift of health care resources from inpatient services to out-of-hospital care. The bailout came in conjunction with a waiver of Medicaid regulations, allowing health care for patients to be contracted out to private managed care organizations.

Medicaid Managed Care (Section 1115 Waiver)

Under the Section 1115 Waiver of the Medicaid law, states can develop a managed care delivery system that expands coverage to include uninsured low-income families and elderly and disabled people. To deliver health services to its enrollees, states contract with the following types of private insurance agencies:

- fee-for-service primary care case management arrangement;
- limited-risk prepaid health plans; and
- full-risk plans (HMOs).

Medicaid patients could select health plans among several plan options. Under the 1115 Waiver, the states regulated the plans and had the ability to set eligibility that could broaden coverage. To comply with federal and state mandates, the health care plans were supposed to emphasize preventive and primary care and reduce the use of hospital services. The Waiver allowed flexibility in the program and used a form of managed competition, attempting to reduce costs by having private health insurance companies compete for contracts and members. Although using this Waiver provided health care coverage to many additional uninsured individuals, it failed in any state to achieve universal coverage. Major problems remained with access to care and quality of care in the Medicaid managed care programs.

I thanked God that finally the dysfunctional reimbursement scheme by which Medi-Cal paid the LAC-DHS would be switched from virtually total reliance on payment per acute-care hospital day to paying per patient insured (i.e., capitated reimbursement). Capitated reimbursement would mean that good pain control and palliative care for the dying would no longer be financial drains, but would become essential components of a marketable health care program. No longer would the reimbursement system favor the hospital's financial bottom line to keep terminally ill patients hospitalized for weeks and months in the final phases of their lives.

In an additional remarkable paradox, the LAC-DHS stepped up its lobbying for a 900-bed replacement hospital for the outmoded LAC+USC Medical Center. Engineers projected an approximately $1.2 billion price tag and seven to nine years before completion. Meanwhile, we were to remain in the old hospital despite numerous building code violations and an operating cost of $700 million per year of which $250 million was solely for plant maintenance. (Appendix #175)

Before the Clinton bailout, Medi-Cal had been paying a bonus to the LAC-DHS for each acute care hospital patient day under the "Disproportionate Share Hospitals" program. In conjunction with the bailout, the LA County Supervisors and Clinton administration health care bureaucrats negotiated an increase to 175% of cost for each hospital day (i.e., over $3,800 per day).

I soon found out that the LAC-DHS would take the bailout money and disregard the strings, requiring a shift of resources to out-of-hospital care.

34

Closure of the Pain and Palliative Care Service

After this dramatic worsening of the already dysfunctional financial incentives from Washington and Sacramento, the LAC-USC Pain and Palliative Care Service (formerly Cancer and AIDS Pain Service) closed in September 1995 with the "downsizing" of the LAC-DHS by 3,000 employees (out of 22,000). LA County administrators agreed to the cuts to win the Clinton financial bailout. The large downsizing of LAC-DHS employees provided the cover so that the closure of the Pain and Palliative Care Service went unchallenged by many of the LAC+USC Medical Center health care workers and the LA County Board of Supervisors.

Dr. Blackhall quit her job with the USC School of Medicine in September 1995 and went into private practice. Dr. Goldstein transferred me to solely supervising internal medicine residents on inpatient wards and in outpatient clinics. (Appendices #145, #146) Management laid off Cadena Bedney, RN, the nurse clinician on the Pain and Palliative Care Service.

In the same downsizing move, they laid off Jonathan Weisbuch, MD, the former LAC-DHS Medical Director and my strongest proponent of expanding palliative care throughout the LAC-DHS. Seeing the writing on the wall, Jay Westbrook, RN, the research nurse for two federally funded pain studies conducted by the Service, quit.

Pain and Palliative Care Service referrals were to be seen by general internal medicine consult residents and staffed by the rotating attending covering general internal medicine. The previous rate of 35–40 referrals per month quickly dwindled to less than five per month as the residents learned that no specialist in palliative care was assigned to the Service.

Dr. Valerie Israel, a recently qualified medical oncologist, was assigned to conduct a half-day clinic in the AIDS building to dispense prescriptions for analgesic medications to AIDS patients. This served to secure funds to the LAC+USC AIDS Clinic, which received over $800 for each pain clinic visit from Medi-Cal. Formerly, the Medical Center lost this revenue whenever I made it convenient for AIDS patients by phoning the orders to outside pharmacies and having the medications delivered to their homes.

Dr. Edward Crandall, the new chief of internal medicine denied my appeal to stay on the Pain and Palliative Care Service.

35

(Appendices #147, #148) My appeal to Dr. Kaufman described what I thought to be the effect on LAC-DHS restructuring of Medi-Cal financial incentives to move to managed care: (Appendix #149)

> In the past, the biggest problem with my treatment of cancer and AIDS patients was that good pain control and palliative care led to fewer acute care hospital days and less Medi-Cal money for the hospital. By all accounts the incentive structure will now be shifted away from inpatient to out-of-hospital care. We will no longer be rewarded for poor palliative care.

I grossly miscalculated the effect of the Clinton bailout on changing the dysfunctional financial incentives driving the hospital.

Dr. Kaufman did not respond to my objection to this reassignment. Mr. Michael Henry, Director of Personnel, fielded my letter to LA County Supervisor Michael Antonovich: (Appendix #150)

> The Department of Health Services has indicated that LAC+USC Medical Center will have available staff to consult regarding difficult cases and on-going education of residents and staff regarding pain control. LAC+USC Medical Center will monitor the adequacy of the pain control program through its quality assurance process and will take appropriate actions to modify the program as necessary within available resources.

The available staff that management referred to in advising Supervisor Antonovich was rotating second and third-year medical residents supervised by 12 rotating general internal medicine faculty members—like the blind leading the blind.

Chapter 5

Letters of Concern and

Poor Performance Evaluations

While on the Cancer and AIDS Pain Service (later called the Pain and Palliative Care Service), I wrote only a few letters of concern to the LAC+USC Quality Assurance (QA) Committee about poor treatment of pain. I did not want to alienate referring physicians, but sometimes I had to speak out. However, after management closed the Pain and Palliative Care Service, I took a suggestion from LA County Supervisor Michael Antonovich's surrogate's letter (Appendix #150) and made a regular practice of recording access to care problems of patients and errors in pain treatment or palliative care, and lodging complaints to the LAC+USC Medical Center QA Committee.

The following case is an example of the 74 cases that I referred to LAC-USC Medical Center Medical Director Dr. Ronald Kaufman and the QA Committee.

By April 1996 I had written 18 letters of concern to the QA Committee, mostly about cases of poor quality treatment of pain. Dr. Kaufman, obviously annoyed by these letters, expressed this in a letter. (Appendix #153) I found it astonishing that the newly formed LAC+USC Ad Hoc Task Force on Pain and Palliative Care dismissed all my letters of concern with the simple statement: (Appendix #153)

> The group met over a period of several months and undertook the evaluation of your concerns by chart (18 individuals) and literature review. The overall conclusions were that the care provided was appropriate in all cases, but identified areas where improvements could be made in both the knowledge and system of care provision.

When I refused to stop writing letters of concern, Dr. Kaufman summoned me to one of the meetings of the Ad Hoc Committee on

Pain and Palliative Care. The notes from the meeting included the following: (Appendix #154)

- My letters of concern pointed to the need for systematic changes in the process for providing pain care.
- My letters demonstrated systemic problems and knowledge deficit problems.
- Reviewing each individual letter of concern was much too time consuming for the Committee.
- More education was required on pain management for the housestaff.
- Practice guidelines were needed for pain management.
- Oncology and Hematology fellows should be given reorientation on pain care for cancer patients.

The notes of the meeting also recorded what I was told verbally, "Committee asked Dr. Cundiff to stop writing referrals and to work together as a team in hopes to achieve resolution and improvement." (Appendix #154)

Because management offered no increase of resources or other tangible means of improving pain control in the hospital, I did not stop writing letters of concern. In a letter dated April 11, 1996 to LAC-DHS Director, Mark Finucane, I requested that he direct my letters of concern to be reviewed by an impartial outside organization such as the Southern California Cancer Pain Initiative to access related letters to QA Committee (Appendix #155 and #155a). He ignored this suggestion but later asked me to meet on October 23, 1996 with William Loos, MD, LAC-DHS Medical Director, about the issue of pain management at the LAC+USC Medical Center. Dr. Loos also advised me to stop writing letters of concern. In his letter regarding the meeting, he said: "As we discussed, it is difficult and potentially misleading to determine the adequacy of pain control at a facility through anecdotal reporting." (Appendix #156)

As my letters of concern continued, Dr. Kaufman warned me about continuing this practice. In a memorandum to me dated November 4, 1996, he cautioned: (Appendix #157)

Letters of Concern and Poor Performance Evaluations

> Your memo identifies your view that some portions of
> this patient's care could have been improved. I feel
> that it is the responsibility of the attending staff to
> communicate these issues among peers within the
> department to maximally benefit our patients. Your
> role as a physician in the facility requires your
> constructive feedback to go back to your peers, to
> instruct the housestaff, and finally to notify your
> Chief, David Goldstein, MD. I feel that this type of
> communication will be most productive if you pursue
> these avenues rather than sending it to me.
> Ultimately, you will decide how best to benefit our
> patients, these are only suggestions.

Given that Department of Health Services Administration had
endorsed Dr. Goldstein's closure of the Pain and Palliative Care
Service, I did not see how my constructive criticism would be well
received by him. Without a consultation service, I had no platform to
provide feedback to my faculty peers or to teach the housestaff other
than to write letters of concern. Even my standard lecture on cancer
and AIDS pain management, that I have given over 300 times in
other hospitals and to outside groups of physicians, had not been
welcomed in medical grand rounds for the 17 years of my tenure at
LAC+USC Medical Center.

Dr. Kaufman repeated this warning to me in memorandums
dated November 20, 1996 (Appendix #158), December 1996, and
September 19, 1997. (Appendix #159)

After over two years of prodding the Administration to improve
pain management services with my letters of concern, no progress was
apparent. The following is an excerpt of a letter I sent to Mark
Finucane, Director of the LAC-DHS, in December 1997, about a man
with severe post-chemotherapy neuropathic pain who could not seem
to get his pain medications from anyone but me: (Appendix #314)

> For the past several months, I have asked Mr. Y. to
> call for an appointment to the Hudson Clinic for us to
> see him and document reasonable monitoring of his
> opioid treatment of pain. It is my professional duty to

do so. He has not been able to schedule an appointment using the appointment number.

Today he came to my office for the triplicate and I asked him to call for an appointment in early January 1998 from my phone. I gave him the number from my database (213-744-3945) to make a Hudson Clinic appointment, and he tried for over 30 minutes without success. He kept getting a recorded message that only led to other options with busy signals. Finally, he succeeded in getting two other numbers to make appointments (213-744-5150 and 213-744-5152). Again, he was led to the same recorded message and finally busy signals.

I called the primary care doctors' office at Hudson Clinic and asked to be put through to the primary care clinic front desk. Ramon, the clerk, could not find any computerized record of Mr. Y's two previous visits to my Hudson Primary Care Clinic. He said that on October 22, 1997, a new patient appointment was made for Mr. Y on April 15, 1998. In order to schedule him an earlier appointment, I would have to speak with Dr. Gelbert, the primary care clinic director. I got Dr. Gelbert's approval for an appointment for January 13, 1998.

This process took the patient and me over an hour to accomplish.

After my departure from the LAC-DHS, this patient's access to treatment for his pain continued to be problematic (Chapter 8).

Poor Performance Evaluation 1993–1997

Beginning in 1979 when I joined the LAC-DHS at Harbor-UCLA Medical Center and Long Beach General Hospital, my yearly evaluations by a variety of raters, including Dr. Goldstein, always showed competent or better until a very unfavorable rating by Dr.

40

Goldstein in 1993–1994. (Appendix #160) He gave me a poor rating in scholarship/research despite the recent publication of a book entitled: *Euthanasia is Not The Answer—A Hospice Physician's View.* Medical and lay critics favorably reviewed this book, including Jonathan Weisbuch, MD, Medical Director of LAC-DHS, until 1994. (Appendix #161) Dr. Goldstein justified my poor rating on citizenship by noting that I did not follow his directives or department policy. The overall evaluation was improvement needed. (Appendix #160) This appeared to be retaliation for using the grievance process to challenge his impossible or unfair directives. I filed a grievance concerning this performance evaluation. (Appendix #162) Dr. Kaufman rescinded it, later saying that it was because Dr. Goldstein used a USC evaluation form instead of an LA County form. (Appendix #164)

Dr. Goldstein's subsequent evaluation of me on the correct LA County form showed an overall competent rating but contained the following comments: "Dr. Cundiff is unable to complete his duties within the normal work day/week. He states that he is not able to take care of all of the cancer pain duties within a 40-hour work week. I have explained that I believe that this is unacceptable and I hope to see a plan for improvement." (Appendix #164) Specifically concerning the Cancer and AIDS Pain Service, he gave me a rating of "improvement needed" saying: "[He] has not created an interdisciplinary approach nor disseminated the management of cancer pain among non-internal medicine faculty." (Appendix #165)

I filed a grievance of the revised performance evaluation, making several points to Dr. Kaufman. My Cancer and AIDS Pain Service rounds were always open to any internal medicine or other faculty—none chose to come. I welcomed residents and fellows from any clinical discipline to do rotations with the Cancer and AIDS Pain Service. With a few exceptions, program chiefs from medical oncology, hematology, radiation therapy, gynecology-oncology, psychiatry, and infectious disease did not encourage or even permit their residents or fellows to do clinical rotations on the Cancer and AIDS Pain Service. Once internal medicine residents began doing Cancer and AIDS Pain Service rotations in conjunction with general internal medicine consults in 1993, they gave high praise to the clinical experience and the teaching.

I could not defend my efficiency in consulting on and following patients referred to the Cancer and AIDS Pain Service to management's satisfaction ostensibly because of the lack of a frame of reference. I started the first Cancer and AIDS Pain Service in the LAC-DHS. Subsequently, none of the other hospitals in the County had developed a similar service. The largest cancer pain service in the United States is located at the Memorial Sloan Kettering Cancer Center (MSKCC) in New York City. In the 1990s, the MSKCC Cancer and AIDS Pain Service averaged about 60 new consults per month. About 20 full-time nurse and physician clinicians and researchers staffed the MSKCC Cancer and AIDS Pain Service.

In contrast, at the LAC+USC Medical Center, one nurse and I saw and followed an average of 20 new patients per month until 1993 and then 35 new patients per month in the latter two years of operation of the Cancer and AIDS Pain Service. Jackie Carter, RN, the nurse clinician of the recently reconstituted anesthesiology-run LAC-DHS Pain Service estimated that in 1998 the new Service saw 25–30 new consults per month. The clinical staffing then included a chief physician, three anesthesiology residents (each working on the Pain Service at least half of their 60+ hour week), a medical social worker, and a registered nurse. That procedure-oriented service did not monitor patients at home.

Dr. Kaufman denied my appeal. (Appendices #165 and #166)

For the evaluation period July 1994–June 1995, Dr. Goldstein again gave me a failing evaluation. He ranked my teaching as "poor" and my clinical care as "fair." (Appendix #167) I filed another grievance (Appendix #168) and Dr. Kaufman rescinded the evaluation. (Appendix #169)

My final evaluation by Dr. Goldstein for the calendar year 1997 found me again with "unsatisfactory" performance. (Appendix #170) My grievance and detailed response (Appendices #171 and #172) was "denied" by Dr. Kaufman, (Appendix #173) yet he significantly revised the performance evaluation and changed the overall rating from unsatisfactory to "competent." (Appendix #174)

Chapter 6

Whistleblowing Activities

In the spring of 1996, I sent Leon Panetta, Chief of Staff in the Clinton Administration, a copy of an alternative LAC-DHS restructuring proposal. I suggested switching to a capitated system of reimbursement for the LAC-DHS so that we would be paid per patient rather than per hospital bed filled. I suggested that we could lease licensed acute-care hospital beds from other hospitals or buy one or two small hospitals rather than spend $900 million–$1.2 billion and seven to nine years to replace the LAC+USC Medical Center.

Mr. Panetta referred the letter to Secretary of Health and Human Services, Donna Shalala, whose assistant, Lu Zawistowich, issued a boiler-plate reply. (Appendix #176 and #177) I posted updated versions of the restructuring proposal to dozens of other health care administrators and politicians. Responses that I received included those of Philip Lee, MD, Assistant Secretary of Health; David Janssen, CAO of LA County Government; Deane Dana, Michael Antonovich, and Gloria Molina, LA County Supervisors; James Rogan, California Assemblyperson; and Stephen Ryan, MD, Dean of the USC School of Medicine. (Appendix #178, #179, #180, #181, #182, #183, #184, and #185) My Congressman, Steven Horn, also graciously met with me concerning restructuring of the LAC-DHS. (Appendix #186)

Appeals to Health Care Administrators and Politicians

On March 19, 1997, I wrote to Mark Finucane, Director of the LAC-DHS, and the five members of the LA County Board of Supervisors arguing that the aging LAC+USC Medical Center should not be replaced. Instead, I suggested leasing inpatient beds, which would free up resources for vastly expanding the health care provided by the LAC-DHS. In this letter I submitted results of an audit of my inpatient medicine ward service consisting of 52 consecutive patients, 15 of which did not require hospitalization or they needed fewer acute-care hospitalization days than they received. (Appendix #189) Mr. Finucane responded: (Appendix #190)

> Most of the cases indicate either problems with obtaining diagnostic tests or inadequate professional resources to deal with the patient-related problems in a timelier manner. It is of the utmost importance that you, as the attending physician, provide the appropriate information to your house staff to ensure efficient and cost-effective evaluation and hospitalization for our patients.
>
> I am totally supportive of the efforts of the Department of Health Services in changing our system into one that is focused on increasing ambulatory care and downsizing our inpatient services. However, I have been disappointed with the response from the private sector in committing to a long-term contract for our patients. I have found that the private sector has beds but not the services that our patients require. I hope that you join with me in supporting an improved health system that provides the right care, at the right time, to the right people.

By focusing on my role to teach the residents to provide timely, cost-efficient care, Mr. Finucane missed my point that the LAC-DHS system-wide policies and procedures supported unnecessary hospital stays IN ORDER TO INCREASE REVENUES. He also dodged my point that the LAC-DHS could lease licensed hospital beds from private facilities for LAC-DHS personnel. Instead, he focused on contracting with private health care providers to provide the care to patients that LAC-DHS employees had been doing.

Supervisor Gloria Molina didn't appear to have read my letter about rampant overutilization of hospital beds and gave me her stump speech on why the LAC-DHS Medical Center replacement project needed to have at least 750 beds. (Appendix #191)

Gina Clemons, the Los Angeles County Project Officer in the federal Medi-Cal program administration, responded to my proposal by saying, "We strongly recommend that you share your suggestions with County officials." (Appendix #192) She either ignored or didn't understand the paradoxical situation of Medi-Cal's method of reimbursing the LAC-DHS that encouraged our wasteful and dysfunctional system. On the phone, she told me that federal health care administrators would only define the goals that the LAC-DHS should achieve in terms of access to health care and efficiency and quality of services. According to Ms. Clemons, federal bureaucrats would not tell Mark Finucane how to "micromanage" the LAC-DHS.

Janet Olsen-Coyle, Chief of the County Waiver Projects in the California State Medi-Cal administration, answered my proposal more affirmatively. She had a particular interest in providing acute care services with public-private partnerships in lieu of building a replacement for LAC+USC Medical Center. (Appendix #193) She invited me to attend the LA County Board of Supervisors meeting November 15, 1997, in which the fate of the LAC+USC Medical Center replacement project would be and was debated in a highly charged atmosphere. I indicated to her that if I had spoken out before such a partisan crowd of replacement project supporters, I would have been lynched. The Supervisors voted to approve a 600-bed replacement hospital over the objections of Supervisor Gloria Molina who insisted on at least 750 beds.

LA Times Editorial against Hospital Replacement

On November 24, 1997, the LA Times published my editorial stating what I had told the Supervisors and Mr. Finucane about the inadvisability of replacing the LAC+USC Medical Center with a $900 million 600-bed hospital or any new public works project. I called for rectifying the perverse financial incentives from Medi-Cal and using the money saved to provide comprehensive health insurance for all LA County's 3 million medical safety net services recipients. (Appendix #194) No one in the LAC-DHS management responded publicly or privately, but I heard several rumors that upper management was furious with me. My subsequent letter to Mr. Finucane listing further patients that had unnecessary days in LAC+USC Medical Center on my service December 1997 was not answered. (Appendix #195)

The Final Audit of My Internal Medicine Service

While attending on the medical wards during the month of February 1998, I did a more extensive analysis of the unnecessary days that my patients spent in hospital and why. I found that 40 out of 104 patients admitted to my service had unnecessary days in the hospital. These superfluous days totaled 28% of the overall patient days in hospital that month. Deficiencies in adequate palliative care services accounted for 28% of the excess days. Delays in a medical subspecialty work-ups explained 17% of the wasted time in hospital. Holdups in the process of placement in a chronic care facility due to social work problems accounted for 12% of the days. About 11% of the unnecessary days were due to waiting in queues for performing surgery. Delays in beginning chemotherapy caused 8% of the needless days. By comparing the average number of days in hospital per admission of my patients and those treated by the entire Department of Medicine, I found that my patients stayed 38% less time than the Department average. (Appendix #196)

I used these figures to estimate what the average hospital occupancy census would be without our institutionalized system of policies and procedures designed to increase the census. From this one-month audit of my inpatient service, I calculated that the average census of patients needing to be in hospital was only 56% of those actually occupying beds. Applying this figure to the $700 million per year operating budget of LAC+USC Medical Center in 1998 (over 80% supplied from Medi-Cal), I made a conservative estimate that my hospital defrauded Medi-Cal out of at least $200 million per year. Then on March 9, 1998, I sent a letter with this analysis to Gina Clemons in the federal Medi-Cal Administration, Janet Olsen-Coyle in the California State Medi-Cal bureaucracy, and 11 Los Angeles area Democrat members of the US House of Representatives. The letter began: (Appendix #197)

> Under the federal false claims act, employees who
> work for companies with federal contracts may bring
> qui tam lawsuits on behalf of the federal government.
> Qui tam suits prosecute fraudulent billing of the
> federal government by private businesses or public
> agencies. I am prepared with documentation to file a

qui tam lawsuit against my employer, the LA
County+USC Medical Center, on behalf of the federal
government. An experienced qui tam attorney is
pursuing the case with me. The contention of my
proposed suit is that the LA County+USC Medical
Center over-bills the federal government by over $200
million per year for unnecessary hospitalization of
Medi-Cal patients.

Ms. Clemons and the 11 Congressmen did not respond to my
letter. Ms. Olsen-Coyle and Republican Pete Wilson's administration
realized the utter waste of a LAC+USC Medical Center replacement
project but feared that forcefully opposing it would alienate the
coalition of LA County's 3 million medically indigent, the LA County
Government employees, and the unions. Ms. Olsen-Coyle got cold feet
at my mention of a qui tam suit. She broke off our communication
and had a Wilson administration legal bureaucrat send me a circuitous
reply. (Appendix #198)

Soaring DHS Hospitalization Costs

A search of the Internet revealed that in 1993, before the federal
bailout, the census for the six LA County public hospitals averaged
2,668 inpatients per day. Revenue that year—almost entirely from
Medi-Cal and other government sources—totaled $1.76 billion or
$1,880 per hospital day. From 1994, when the federal bailout was
negotiated, until 1998 the daily census plummeted to 1,776 while
revenues swelled—due to government bonus payments
(Disproportionate Share Hospital funds)—to $3,360 per day (a 79%
increase).[1] This translates into about $1 billion per year more going to
DHS hospitals than would have been paid with 1993 rates.

Using the results of my audit of medically unnecessary inpatient
days at the LAC+USC Medical Center, the cost of each medically
necessary day in LAC-DHS hospitals would be about $6,000
($3,360/0.56 = $6,000). This compares with $1,465 per day revenues
for the average day in all California hospitals in 1997. While LAC-
DHS hospital administrators were desperately trying to raise the
census of their hospitals, LAC-DHS Director Mark Finucane and
upper level management reported the opposite to the media. They

said that reducing hospital census showed that the Department of Health Services was complying with the bailout conditions to shift resources from hospitals to out-of-hospital care.

The dramatic increase in acute care payments for LAC-DHS inpatient care made it self-defeating for Mr. Finucane and his colleagues to comply with the mandate to shift resources from hospitals to outpatient care. This doomed his plans to reengineer the LAC-DHS by shifting resources from inpatient to outpatient by paying even more handsomely for any inefficiency that kept patients in County hospitals for as long as possible. This obscenely high government reimbursement for hospitalization of medically indigent patients also drove LAC-DHS health care administrators and some LA County politicians to push for the largest replacement hospital possible for the LAC+USC Medical Center.

Los Angeles County has about 20,000 licensed acute-care hospital beds that average about 50% occupied. The number of acute-care days in hospital decreased by about 14% from 1992 to 1997. The number of licensed acute care beds continued to fall as managed care financial incentives become universal. Comparing 2001 with 2006 (the last year with available data) at the LAC+USC Medical Center, the census dropped 8% and the cost per inpatient per day increased 37%. The cost per inpatient day was $3,936 ($919,171,842 total operating costs[1]/233,576 inpatient days = $3,936 per inpatient day). Moving terminally ill patients to inpatient hospices or to home hospice care would be more financially devastating now for the LAC-USC Medical Center than in the 1990s.

Distinction between Waste and Fraud

After extensively investigating the possibility of filing a "whistleblower" lawsuit against the LAC-DHS for defrauding the Medi-Cal program, I found that the federal and state "False Claims Acts" (i.e., qui tam laws) make a distinction between waste and fraud. Legally, institutionalized inefficiency designed to maximize reimbursement does not qualify as fraud. Apparently, the highly dysfunctional structure of the LAC-DHS and the extremely high reimbursement per hospital day granted by the Clinton administration, and subsequently the Bush and Obama administrations, to prevent the bankruptcy of LA County meet all the relevant laws and regulations of the federal and state Medicaid program.

Chapter 7

Getting Fired

About six-weeks after my op-ed piece appeared in the *LA Times*, Dr. Goldstein called me to his office to discuss eight issues related to my behavior and performance. (Appendices #199, #200, #201) I filed a grievance about the seven charges that were unfair (Appendices #202, #203), and included copious documentation. (Appendices #204, #205, #206, #207, #208, #209, #210, #211, #212, #213, #214, #215, #216, #217, #218, #219, #220, #221, #222) Dr. Kaufman denied it on all seven issues that I disputed. (Appendix #223) The utter lack of merit of these seven charges and the backup of senior LAC+USC Medical Center management made it obvious to me that they would use any means available to get me fired.

On March 13, 1998, Dr. Goldstein took me off of all clinical duties and put me on paid administrative leave (Appendix #224) only stating, "Based on recent peer review findings, I have decided to reassign you until further notice to non-patient care activity pending further administrative review." As revealed by other documents given to me later by Dr. Goldstein, the administrative process leading to my reassignment followed an interesting time sequence. On February 27, 1998, Dr. Goldstein wrote me a memorandum assigning me to administrative leave, but did not have upper management authorization to send it. (Appendix #225) Then on March 2, 1998, a peer review committee report concerning two of my patients went to Dr. Goldstein. (Appendix #226) On March 9, 1998, I posted the letter leveling my strongest yet criticism of the LAC-DHS to federal and state Medicaid administrators and 11 Democratic Congress Members, accusing the LAC-DHS of defrauding Medicaid out of over $200 million per year. (Appendix #227) On March 11, 1998, Dr. Goldstein sent Dr. Kaufman a memorandum recommending that I be terminated. (Appendix #228) Two days later, Dr. Goldstein got the go ahead to put me on administrative leave, but not to send me an "intent to terminate letter." (Appendix #224)

While on paid administrative leave for 5-1/2 months, I worked on a new book entitled: *Money Driven Medicine – Tests and Treatments*

That Don't Work. A USC medical student and I also submitted a letter to the editor entitled: "Meperidine versus Morphine in Pancreatitis and Cholecystitis," which was accepted by the *Archives of Internal Medicine.* (Appendices #220 and #221) Dr. Goldstein had denied my request to use LAC+USC Medical Center stationery to send the manuscript. (Appendix #222)

In the beginning of August 1998, Daniel Jones, an HIV-infected man, appalled the world with his televised suicide. He shot himself in the head on a Los Angeles freeway to dramatize the deficiencies in his medical treatment, specifically his undertreated pain.[1] I submitted an op-ed piece to the *LA Times* on this case, which the op-ed editor told me was accepted and just awaited editing. (Appendix #238) However, after several weeks it became obvious that the *Times* editors would never print it.

Management's intent to terminate letter came to me August 27, 1998 with the signature of Albert Niden, MD, Associate Chair of Internal Medicine for County Affairs. (Appendix #229) At that time Dr. Goldstein gave me a copy of a peer review report that found me guilty of "substandard care" involving two more patients in January and February of 1998. (Appendix #226) Dr. Niden highlighted one of those patients in the intent to terminate letter (Appendix #229). In the other case, Dr. Goldstein assessed the peer review committee finding and concluded: "There is insufficient documentation regarding patient (HHH) to warrant disciplinary action." (Appendix #228)

Management did not mention the second patient (Appendix #226) or the eight issues entered into my record in January 1998 as justification for my termination from County service. This second case of alleged "substandard care" on my part illustrated the problem with care of the dying at LAC+USC Medical Center and at many other hospitals throughout the country. I will describe the details of this case.

Morphine Pump for Treatment of Bone Pain

A medicine consultation team under my supervision saw Mr. HHH, a 64-year-old man, in January 1998. Mr. HHH had been bed bound and a long-term resident of a nursing home. He had dementia and multiple other medical problems, including an infected hip prosthesis for which he was admitted to the orthopedic service. His nutritional state manifested by a serum albumin of 1.0 mg/dl (normal range is 3.5-5.0 mg/dl) was so low that he would be very unlikely to heal a wound after surgery. Because of his dementia and poor nutritional state, I suggested that the patient receive only palliative treatment without submitting him to the risk and suffering of a major surgical intervention.

Because of the patient's pain, I recommended a patient-controlled analgesia pump to give a constant morphine infusion plus boluses of morphine by the nurses whenever Mr. HHH appeared to have breakthrough pain. During the first night the patient's blood pressure fell to the range of 80/40 and the on-call resident discontinued the pump. The next day my resident and I assessed that the low blood pressure (hypotension) had occurred because the orthopedic doctors had so aggressively diuresed the patient (i.e., used medication to remove excess fluid) that he had become dehydrated. Infusing 13 mg of morphine in 7-1/2 hours was not the primary cause of the hypotension. The orthopedic team agreed to resume the morphine via PCA pump on the following afternoon, but did not rehydrate the patient. Again the patient became hypotensive and the orthopedic resident stopped the PCA pump. The patient suffered no adverse consequence due to the morphine infusion.

The orthopedic attending thought that morphine alone was to blame for the low blood pressure and took me off of the case. They continued with intensive treatment to prepare the patient for hip surgery. Mr. HHH had the operation, but remained febrile and presumably infected for the remainder of the hospitalization. He resided in the intensive care unit for most of his three-month hospitalization. His family was increasingly upset about his terrible suffering throughout the prolonged ordeal. He died in the nursing home shortly after discharge. The peer review committee determined that my recommendation of using the PCA pump for pain control was "not appropriate and deficient in the areas of knowledge, behavior and performance."

Futile treatment in this patient's hospitalization caused great suffering for this man and his family and cost Medi-Cal over $300,000.

The Charges Supporting Termination

By analyzing the seven specific charges cited and the items conspicuously omitted from the evidence used to support firing me, I could see how desperate management had become to stifle my dissenting voice about the LAC-DHS deficiencies in palliative care and the need for a completely new direction in reengineering the LAC-DHS. Only one of the seven charges was an allegation of medical malpractice.

I will begin with the medical malpractice allegation and enumerate the other six incidents referenced in the final termination letter dated October 15, 1998. (Appendix #230)

Item #1: Thromboembolism Case—"Below Standard Care."

An outside hospital transferred a 59-year-old black man to my inpatient medicine service for treatment of tuberculosis and deep venous thrombosis of the popliteal vein (vein behind the knee). He died of massive pulmonary emboli (clots that traveled from the leg to the lung) seven days after I had discontinued the anticoagulant medications. I deeply regret that this patient died. This very complex judgment call involved a situation with a significant chance of death with either course of action.

My expert witness, Dr. Matthew Conolly, Professor of Medicine at UCLA Medical Center, and I surveyed 101 California internal medicine specialists and anticoagulation experts on how they would manage this patient's deep venous thrombosis treatment (TheHealthEconomy.com/ChaptersMDM.pdf pages 407–418). The survey showed no uniformity of opinion among doctors about the proper treatment. Significant numbers of internists and anticoagulation specialists chose each of the five suggested treatment options, including 12/101 (12%) who would have stopped Coumadin as I did. Most internists and thromboembolic disease specialists (both 89%) thought that some or all treatment choices other than the one(s) they selected represented malpractice. Seven percent of the physicians chose the same treatment option as their recommended treatment as

54

they designated as "below standard care" (malpractice). They indicated that their own preferred treatment option was malpractice.

My research of the treatment of venous thromboembolism (VTE: deep venous thrombosis or DVT and pulmonary emboli or PE) revealed that the standard anticoagulant treatment is based on historical precedent and a consensus of anticoagulation experts, virtually all with financial conflicts of interest, rather than solid scientific clinical trials. http://www.medscape.com/viewarticle/487577). I coauthored a review of the treatment of VTE in the prestigious *Cochrane Library of Systematic Reviews*.[2] However, the *Cochrane* peer-reviewers and editor changed the interpretation of the data, overruling me and the other authors. My formal complaint to *Cochrane* about the peer-reviewer biases and undisclosed financial conflicts of interest, lodged in September 2006, has still not been addressed. (http://medgenmed.medscape.com/viewarticle/557263)

Item #2: Letters of Concern Regarding Pain

Dr. Goldstein documented the second incident in a memorandum, dated July 3, 1997, concerning: ". . . your inability to work effectively with physicians and your continuing to perform work in the area of pain management consultation after being told to cease this activity." This issue arose after I wrote two letters of concern. One letter concerned Mr. JJJ, a 45-year-old colon cancer patient that my medical team transferred to the surgery service. I continued to follow the patient and criticized the surgeons' management of pain. (Appendix #233) This letter generated an outraged reply from the attending surgeon that I mentioned in the letter. (Appendix #234)

Dr. Goldstein declared that it was "unprofessional conduct" for me to continue to follow Mr. JJJ from my medical service with cancer-related pain after he was transferred to a surgery team. (Appendix #235) Dr. Goldstein said that continuing to follow Mr. JJJ regarding the treatment of pain violated his directive when he transferred me from the Pain and Palliative Care Service to supervising ward admitting residents.

I worried that Mr. JJJ would get inadequate medication for the pain. Indeed, according to the dutifully recorded records of the nurses, they did not effectively treat his pain. I tried to educate the surgeons about the treatment of pain on behalf of Mr. JJJ. The surgeons were unreceptive and Mr. JJJ continued with uncontrolled pain. My letter of concern to the Quality Assurance Committee represented an attempt to focus the attention of the surgeons on the issue of adequate treatment of pain.

Ms. BB

The second case referred to by Dr. Goldstein regarding the unprofessional conduct charge concerned Ms. BB, a 41-year-old woman, who came to my inpatient medicine service with a severe calf abscess from injecting heroin with dirty needles. After I transferred Ms. BB to orthopedics for an incision and drainage, I found that the orthopedic doctors were not controlling her pain. I wrote a letter of concern to the Quality Assurance Committee after a direct discussion with the leaders of the orthopedic service, which did not result in better pain treatment. (Appendix #207) Dr. Goldstein used their angry letters in response (Appendices #208, #209, and #210) to justify charging me with unprofessional conduct. (Appendix #235) No one responded to my rebuttal. (Appendix #211)

In these cases and in several others related to this action, the Quality Assurance Committee did not evaluate my letters of concern, but management allowed the rebuttal letters of the people involved and related correspondence to remain in my permanent personnel file. This violated any semblance of a fair peer review process.

My refusal to stop writing letters of concern when I observed poor treatment of pain was the apparent basis of Dr. Goldstein's assessment that I did not get along with my colleagues. This represented management retaliating against me for fulfilling my obligation to report poor quality medical care.

Items #3–5 of the charges supporting my termination concerned memorandums entitled: "Written Warning/Future Activities," "Disregarding a Direct Order . . .," and "Attending/Rounding on Ward," were discussed in Chapter 3.

Item #6: An AIDS Patient with Pain

A reprimand from Dr. Goldstein, dated November 20, 1995, concerned Mr. EEE, an AIDS patient with severe pain due to soft tissue inflammation and nerve damage. (Appendix #240)

When I was taken off the Pain and Palliative Care Service, I transferred the care of Mr. EEE to Valerie Israel, DO. She attempted to reduce the medication and then became unavailable to Mr. EEE for refills. Mr. EEE called me for help. I phoned Dr. Israel and got an answering machine with no pager number or option for backup assistance if she were unavailable. I left a message on the answer machine that she never returned. The AIDS clinic staff told me that she was out of town. I gave Mr. EEE a one-week emergency prescription of pain medication and indicated this in his chart. (Appendix #241) On Dr. Israel's return, she complained. (Appendix #242) Dr. Goldstein again assessed my actions as unprofessional conduct. (Appendix #240) My explanation and appeal to the Quality Assurance Committee and Dr. Kaufman went unheeded. (Appendix #243)

Item #7: An AIDS Patient Cytomegalovirsus Colitis

Also in November 1995, Mr. Z, a 35-year-old AIDS patient, arrived on my ward medicine service with a history of four months of severe abdominal pain and diarrhea due to cytomegalovirus (CMV) colitis. I immediately ordered long-acting morphine, which controlled both the pain and the diarrhea. Because Mr. Z's pain had been undertreated in the AIDS clinic for four months, I wrote a letter of concern to the Quality Assurance Committee. (Appendix #244)

To determine optimal overall treatment of the CMV colitis, I conducted a computerized literature search that revealed that the standard antiviral agent used against CMV retinitis (eye infection), gancyclovir, was not proven to be effective in CMV colitis cases. The AIDS clinic staff wanted to begin Mr. Z on daily intravenous gancyclovir for the rest of his life. (Appendix #245) I did not prescribe it.

I discussed the case with Robert Larsen, MD, infectious disease ward attending, before discharging Mr. Z from my service. Dr. Larsen agreed with my suggested plan of symptomatic treatment of the pain and diarrhea with morphine alone in light of the absence of evidence that gancyclovir or any other antiviral medication provides any symptomatic or survival benefit in CMV colitis. If he hadn't agreed with my plan, I would have immediately transferred Mr. Z to his service.

Dr. Goldstein asked me to explain myself (Appendix #247), and I did. (Appendix #248) The Quality Assurance Committee never made an official determination in this case. Despite the absence of an official report on my complaint to the Quality Assurance Committee regarding the dispute, Dr. Goldstein determined that my actions constituted unprofessional conduct and entered his opinion into my personnel file for eventual use to support my termination from County service. (Appendix #249) Dr. Kaufman did not respond to my letters appealing Dr. Goldstein's determination. (Appendices #250 and #251)

Each time I defended myself of malpractice allegations in grievance hearings in the past, management would deny my grievance. YET NONE OF THE PREVIOUS CLINICAL CASES ALLEGING MALPRACTICE WERE MENTIONED IN THE TERMINATION NOTICE. To me it appeared that they were fishing for a cause to fire me, and this one case (Item #1) of my stopping the anticoagulant Coumadin was the best that they could do.

Management allowed me to have from August 27, 1998 until October 1, 1998 to prepare my case to appeal to them. (Appendix #252) However, they did not permit my request for a change of venue so that administrators from another LAC-DHS hospital might decide my fate. After extensively researching the anticoagulants for deep venous thrombosis issue on which my termination was based (Item #1) and finding my clinical decision to stop Coumadin highly defendable, I decided to waive the hearing before the LAC+USC management. I did not want to give Dr. Goldstein and the other administrators my defense.

I feared that this action to fire me was calculated by management to end up short of suspension, resulting in a disciplinary transfer out of the LAC+USC Medical Center. It seemed to be another attempt to intimidate me in order to stop my outspoken criticism of poor pain management and the misguided LAC-DHS reengineering strategy.

I figured that it would be better to be fired and appeal to LA County Civil Service Court than to reach a settlement with management on its terms. The importance of the welfare of LAC-DHS patients justified any personal sacrifice on my part. After I waived the intradepartmental appeal, management took another three weeks to fire me.

Awaiting Termination from LAC+USC Medical Center

During these three weeks, several of my chronic pain patients called me for opioid refills. I did my best to help them get their medication from the medical clinic attendings. This generally failed.

Dr. Goldstein discovered that I was prescribing for Mr. I, a man with severe degeneration of the left hip (avascular necrosis). I had previously written seven letters to Dr. Kaufman on behalf of Mr. I. (Appendices #253, #254, #255, #256, #257, #258, and #259) Dr. Goldstein threatened to add another insubordination charge to the articles supporting my termination because he previously ordered me not to participate in patient care. (Appendix #224) On my final day of employment, I documented the difficulties of Mr. I and four other pain patients who were to be followed by primary care doctors without pain specialist supervision. (Appendices #260, #269, and #357) Mr. I's problems with access to his pain medications continued after my departure from LAC+USC Medical Center. In November 1998 and again in January 1999, I wrote to LA County Supervisor Gloria Molina in his behalf, but she only referred me back to Dr. Kaufman. In June 1999, Mr. I again contacted me because Dr. Kaufman and Dr. Goldstein had written him a letter that said that he was no longer welcome to receive medical care at LAC+USC.

Dr. Goldstein admonished me for writing a pain medication prescription for a patient who could not get one from other LAC+USC physicians. He said: (Appendix #324)

> Should a LAC+USC Medical Center patient contact you regarding any matter, please advise the patient that you cannot treat him and/or her or issue a prescription. . . . If the patient calls after regular working hours, have the patient call Ms. Barrera (Outpatient Department Administrator) on the following work day. In the event

of a patient emergency after working hours, the patient
should be sent to the LAC+USC Department of
Emergency Medicine. . . ."

Such was to be the management of severe pain from cancer and
AIDS on my departure.

Since a very large part of management's case supporting my
termination stems from reactions to my letters of concern about
patient care issues, I will include the rest of these letters that I sent to
management from 1995 to 1998:

1. A ward clerk from Women's Hospital ward clerk told me
   about a cervix cancer patient in pain and no pain consult
   service to call. (Appendix #261)
2. A relative of a patient with colon cancer pain called because
   she could find no one to write prescriptions for opioid pain
   medicine. (Appendix #261)
3. A testis cancer patient with post chemotherapy neuropathic
   pain whose physician went on vacation leaving no one to write
   prescriptions for pain medications. (Appendix #261)
4. A patient with tongue cancer admitted to my service for pain
   out of control. The oncology doctors had reduced the previous
   pain medication doses that were working. (Appendix #262)
5. A patient admitted to my service with pain out of control
   from spinal metastases from a cancer of unknown origin.
   Previous physicians had prescribed inappropriately.
   (Appendix #262)
6. An AIDS patient with peripheral neuropathy pain admitted
   to my service with opioid induced constipation. Previous
   doctors had not ordered laxatives or monitored the patient.
   (Appendix #263)
7. A bladder cancer patient with uncontrolled pain from pelvic
   metastases undertreated by the anesthesiology pain service.
   The oncology consultant did not address the pain. (Appendix
   #264)
8. A lymphoma patient with problems having his pain
   medications refilled. (Appendix #265)
9. Two patients who could not get pain service appointment
   because the doctor was on vacation. (Appendix #266)

10. A medical intern who could find no one to write for pain medications for his patient with pancreatic cancer. (Appendix #267)
11. An AIDS patient with undertreated chronic head pain. (Appendix #268)
12. An AIDS patient with neuropathic pain and problems with timely access to pain medications. (Appendix #269)
13. A call from the emergency room about a patient followed by the Anesthesia Pain Service. (Appendix #270)
14. A lung cancer patient with under treatment of his pain and over treatment of his terminal disease. (Appendix #271)
15. An ovarian cancer patient taken off of pain medications by the gynecological oncologists. (Appendix #272)
16. A lung cancer patient with delay of radiation therapy to a painful area. (Appendix #272)
17. A lung cancer patient on my inpatient service who did not receive the ordered pain medications. (Appendix #273)
18. My patient with esophageal cancer given inadequate pain treatment by other services. (Appendix #274)
19. A lung cancer patient admitted to my service with a fecal impaction and pain out of control. (Appendix #275)
20. A multiple myeloma patient readmitted to my internal medicine service after inadequate palliative care by the Hematology Service. (Appendix #276)
21. A patient with ischemic colitis pain (abdominal pain from lack of blood) and dementia inadequately palliated by the surgeons. (Appendix #276)
22. A man with no continuity of care in the treatment of his severe chronic back pain. (Appendix #277)
23. A lung cancer patient with undertreatment of his pain and overtreatment of his cancer. (Appendix #278)
24. Cancer patient with no doctor available to write for pain medications. (Appendix #279)
25. Gallbladder cancer patient with no outpatient monitoring of symptoms and medications. (Appendix #280)
26. A liver cancer patient with inadequate pain treatment and poor palliative care. (Appendix #281)

27. A sickle cell anemia patient with chronic pain and no one available to write prescriptions for his pain medications. (Appendix #282)

28. Inadequate treatment of pain from advanced cervix cancer. (Appendix #283)

29. An AIDS patient prescribed insufficient medication to control pain from a rectal fissure. (Appendix #284)

30. Treatment of a patient with ovarian cancer pain by residents with inadequate training in cancer pain management. (Appendix #285)

31. An AIDS patient with pneumocystis pneumonia on a ventilator in the intensive care unit with great pain and suffering. (Appendix #286)

32. Poor pain management of a patient with advanced leiomyosarcoma. (Appendix #287)

33. Chinese non-English speaking woman with poorly treated lung cancer pain. (Appendix #288)

34. A multiple myeloma patient with undertreated pain. (Appendix #289)

35. A breast cancer patient with inadequate pain management and palliative care. (Appendix #290)

36. A liver cancer patient with poor pain and symptom management. (Appendix #291)

37. A cancer patient with poorly controlled pain on a colleague's medical service. (Appendix #292)

38. Poor pain management and palliative care for a breast cancer patient. (Appendix #293)

39. Lymphoma patient on opioid pain medication not given laxatives to prevent constipation. (Appendix #294)

40. A chronic pancreatitis patients whose physician had no triplicate prescriptions to order pain medications. (Appendix #295)

41. A stomach cancer patient with poor pain management and inadequate palliative care. (Appendix #296)

42. A lymphoma patient with undertreated pain asked to sign up for an experimental chemotherapy regime and told that improved pain control is a possible benefit. (Appendix #297)

43. An AIDS patient with inadequate management of pain from shingles. (Appendix #298)

44. Poor treatment of hip fracture pain in a patient on the Orthopedic Service. (Appendix #299)
45. An AIDS patient with meningitis pain untreated. (Appendix #300)
46. A bladder cancer patient with undertreated pain. (Appendix #301)
47. A lung cancer patient on the Medical Oncology Service with inadequately treated pain. (Appendix #302)
48. A rectal cancer patient on the Medical Oncology Service with poor pain management. (Appendix #303)
49. An issue of the authority of the primary care physician versus a consultant in considering a cardiac catherization. (Appendix #304)
50. A colon cancer patient treated inadequately for pain. (Appendix 305)
51. Poor pain control and palliative care in an end-stage AIDS patient. (Appendix #306)
52. A lung and colon cancer patient with pain not addressed by Medical Oncology. (Appendix #307)
53. A lymphoma patient with a heroin addiction history inadequately treated for pain by the Hematology Service. (Appendix #308)
54. A breast cancer patient with poor pain management. (Appendix #309)
55. A pancreas cancer patient with poor palliative care. (Appendix #310)
56. An AIDS patient inappropriately admitted to my inpatient service. (Appendix #311)
57. A lung cancer patient with poor pain and symptom management. (Appendix #312)
58. A patient with bilateral hip pain due to avascular necrosis not treated for pain. (Appendix #313)
59. A patient with a failed total hip replacement and delayed reoperation. (Appendix #315)
60. A terminally ill cancer patient abandoned by a for-profit hospice. (Appendix #316)
61. An AIDS patient with brain lymphoma undertreated for pain and overtreated for the lymphoma. (Appendix #317)

62. An AIDS patient resuscitated against his will. (Appendix #318)
63. A man with reflex sympathetic dystrophy and a 10+ week delay in getting into the LAC+USC Pain Clinic. (Appendix #319)
64. A man with advanced cancer of the pancreas who was given inadequate follow-up care. (Appendix #320)

I referred all 83 cases to the complaint section of the Medical Board of California. (Appendix #325, #326, and #327) They said that they would not investigate because the patient or family member has to make the complaint. These patients were almost all dead, and I had no access to their charts to contact the families.

Chapter 8

Awaiting Civil Service Hearing Appealing Termination

After my termination on October 21, 1998, I had to wait until April 27, 1999 for my Civil Service appeal hearing. The outcome of the hearing required a further six-week wait. I welcomed the time to write this book and to pursue treatments to strengthen my low back. Part of that effort was to go to Honduras with a delegation of physicians to learn about "prolotherapy"—injecting inflammation-producing substances to strengthen lax ligaments and tendons of people with chronic musculo-skeletal pain. This treatment had given me a reprieve from my hip and back pain in 1995 before severe nerve entrapment necessitated low-back surgery for spinal stenosis the next year.

While I was getting ready for my appeal, several of my former patients continued to have difficulty receiving opioid pain medications and called for my help.

Mr. BBB—An AIDS Patient with Peripheral Nerve Pain

In 1988, shortly after the initiation of the Cancer and AIDS pain service, an AIDS clinic physician referred Mr. BBB (Appendix #260, #269, and #356) to me for better control of lower body pain from combined HIV and diabetic neuropathy. Mr. BBB was in his early 30s, a well-educated, upper middle class, gay man who had previously worked as a musician, salesman, and other jobs. He denied ever using recreational drugs and had not been in trouble with the law.

At the time I first saw Mr. BBB, he had suffered for more than two years with incapacitating tingling and stabbing and shooting pain from his feet up to his legs (neuropathic pain). None of the medications he received had given any relief of his pain. His quality of life was so poor he believed that he had only a few short months to live.

During the first year of treating Mr. BBB, I tried many pain medicines (analgesics and co-analgesics), including amitriptyline, nortriptyline, valproic acid, mexilitine, salsalate, long-acting morphine, methadone, and Dilaudid. It quickly became apparent that only high doses of opioids—long-acting morphine and Dilaudid— could control the severe neuropathic pain. Once the pain was continuously controlled, his severe depression lifted and he again returned to full activity as the conservator of a relative's sizable will.

The passing of many of his friends and former lovers made him acutely aware of his own mortality, so he resolved to make the most of every remaining day of his life. He traveled to Japan to study Buddhism. He sent me postcards from the hot-air balloon championships in New Mexico. He visited the Caribbean, Hawaii, Europe, and numerous other places.

On one occasion, when returning to the United States from the Caribbean, he was jailed when he showed the customs inspector his Dilaudid bottle complete with the pharmacy label, including my name as his doctor. I had to phone the narcotics policeman to attest to the fact that I prescribed the opioid medication for his severe nerve pain. For a time he was able to return to playing guitar in a band that briefly performed in Spain. Following that he worked as a salesman in a music store.

From the first year, Mr. BBB required about 40 Dilaudid 4mg tablets and about 6–10 long-acting morphine 100mg tablets per day. Other regimes either had incapacitating side effects or were ineffective in controlling his pain. After several years, I discontinued the long-acting morphine at his request and he used only Dilaudid. I continued this pain control regime for Mr. BBB until 1995 when his primary care AIDS doctor took over prescribing the same thing.

In early 1998, his primary care AIDS doctor required an extended medical leave and asked that I resume the role of prescribing his opioids. It seemed that no other physician in the AIDS clinic was comfortable with prescribing this high a dose of Dilaudid for chronic HIV-related pain. During this period, he developed septicemia from a skin infection and almost died. Three days after his admission to an outside hospital in coma and on a mechanical respirator in an intensive care unit, his mother called to ask for my help. Mr. BBB was waking up with severe pain and his new doctors would not give him Dilaudid or any other opioid pain medication. I called to the new doctors, gave them the history of his previous long history of requiring opioids, and recommended that they restart the Dilaudid.

They did so reluctantly and at about one third the previous dose, but he was grateful for the partial relief. On discharge from hospital, I resumed him on the previous Dilaudid dose.

In the spring of 1999, when I was no longer employed by LAC-DHS, Mr. BBB called me to ask for an emergency order of the Dilaudid because he ran out before his appointment with his primary care doctor. His doctor was on vacation and no one else in the clinic would write for the medication. I told him that, due to my pending litigation with LAC-DHS, I didn't want to get involved unless he tried every other alternative. Subsequently, he brought his attorney and his mother to the AIDS clinic and threatened a lawsuit if he didn't get the medication. Finally, the AIDS clinic administration called in his vacationing doctor who wrote for the medication.

After this confrontation, the LAC+USC AIDS clinic administration decided to taper Mr. BBB off of Dilaudid. His primary care physician of 11 years declined to order more Dilaudid for him and referred him to another AIDS clinic physician who had taken some courses and become a "specialist in pain." According to Mr. BBB, this physician reduced Dilaudid dose from 400 tablets each 10-days to 150 tablets every two weeks without even asking how the lower dose was working for the pain.

Since no one was willing to help him at the LAC+USC Medical Center, Mr. BBB found another physician in private practice that was willing to continue the Dilaudid at the regular dose. A couple of years later, his mother called to tell me that he had died from complications of AIDS and hepatitis C and to thank me for treating his pain.

Mr. Y—Post Chemotherapy Pain

Mr. Y was referred to the Cancer and AIDS Pain Service in 1991 because of severe pain in his feet after curative chemotherapy for testicular cancer. The nonopioid pain medications for his kind of nerve pain either did not help or made him sick. I prescribed long-acting morphine along with amitriptyline, which controlled his pain well enough for him to return to normal activities.

Several times Mr. Y lost his medication or used it up faster than I had prescribed. After several years, I switched him to methadone. He stuck to the prescribed dose much more reliably and was satisfied with the control of his foot pain.

When I was removed from the Pain and Palliative Care Service in 1995, his new pain doctor insisted that he be tapered off of the methadone and take only nonopioid medications. (Appendix #261, case 3). Mr. Y asked for my help. I arranged for him to be treated by a hospice physician who was in private practice. After about a year, he returned to me as a patient in one of my general internal medicine clinics. I resumed responsibility for prescribing his pain medications. Even under clinic care that I supervised, access to appointments was very difficult. (Appendix #314)

When I was placed on administrative leave and subsequently fired by the LAC-DHS, Mr. Y continued to receive methadone for several months from the clinic doctor. However, his ongoing problems with access to pain medications led me to write another complaint letter to Dr. Kaufman and quality assurance on October 21, 1998, my last day of County service. (Appendix #260, case 4).

In early 1999, Mr. Y's internal medicine clinic doctor referred him to the Pain Clinic run by the anesthesiology department. The doctor stated that methadone and any other opioid medication was unnecessary—she wrote for only about half the previous methadone dose. When Mr. Y ran out of pain medication early, he phoned to ask for my help. I wrote him a two-week supply to give him time to find another doctor.

Mr. Y wrote LAC-DHS Director Mark Finucane about his continuing problems with accessing care at Hudson Clinic. (Appendix #328. Replying for Mr. Finucane, Roberto Rodriguez, Executive Director of the LAC+USC Healthcare Network, gave a typical bureaucrat's answer. (Appendix #329)

Applying to City of Hope

Shortly after being fired from the Pain and Palliative Care Service in 1995, I launched a job search, looking for positions in palliative care in the local managed care organizations. The prospects were fairly bleak. One personnel officer asked me to spell "palliative care" and then asked what a palliative care specialist did. The very limited number of hospice physician work involved home visits and seeing patients in nursing homes.

A colleague physician at the City of Hope Medical Center suggested that I apply there to head the pain and palliative care service. The previous palliative care specialist had left about one year previously, leaving a reluctant neurologist in charge of cancer pain treatment. The interviews with John Kovacs, MD, the medical director, and several of the faculty went well. But no offer came. I found later that they decided not to hire a pain and palliative care specialist.

Three years later (after being fired by the LAC-DHS), the same colleague suggested that I inquire again about joining the City of Hope as a pain and palliative care specialist. Although no position was officially available, Dr. Kovacs again granted me an interview. I told him about the financial disincentive to hospice care that led to my termination at the LAC-DHS. He said that managed care contracts had led to capitation of reimbursement for about two-thirds of the City of Hope cancer patient population. This meant that, unlike with previous fee-for-service funding, it was now to the hospital's disadvantage to have terminally ill patients linger for weeks and months in hospital before dying. He felt certain that improving the pain treatment and palliative care would not only help patient care, but also help the hospital's financial bottom line. Additionally, the City of Hope's new chief executive officer made it his number one priority to improve palliative care at the hospital. At the end of the interview, Dr. Kovacs assured me that he could find me a position.

Two weeks later when no call or letter came, I followed up with a call that was not returned. It seemed that my reputation with the LAC-DHS had blackballed my chances with the City of Hope.

Doctor Sued For Undertreating Cancer Pain

In January 1999, *Dateline NBC* news magazine, the *New York Times* and other newspapers reported on the case of an 85-year-old man with increasingly severe back pain admitted to a California hospital for treatment.[1] The chest x-ray done in the emergency room revealed a probable lung cancer with spine metastases. His doctor prescribed meperidine (Demerol) injection each four hours as needed for the pain. According to the nurses who carefully assessed and documented the pain treatment, it didn't work. After five days in hospital, the pain was worse than on the first day.

Demerol is not recommended for the treatment of chronic cancer pain because it is too short acting and requires injections. A medical student and I coauthored a letter to the editor published by the *Archives of Internal Medicine* that detailed the problems with Demerol. (Appendix #220)

On discharge from the hospital, the doctor prescribed Vicodan pills, the same pain medication that previously had not worked before the patient came to the hospital. The gentleman suffered unspeakable pain for over another week before a hospice physician was called in to order morphine on the day before the patient died.

With the assistance of Compassion in Dying, an organization that advocates legalization of physician-assisted suicide, and Ira Byock, MD, author of *Dying Well* and spokesperson for hospice, the family brought a complaint to the Medical Board of California. The written response of the Medical Board acknowledged that the physician had grossly undertreated the patient's severe pain. However, it said that no disciplinary action would be taken.

The near absence of clinical training in cancer and AIDS pain management in teaching hospitals like the LAC+USC Medical Center results in poor pain treatment for every stratum of society. Rich people can suffer in private hospitals every bit as much as my poor, medically indigent County patients.

Volunteering in a Clinic for the Poor

In order to keep up my primary care medical skills and help with the care of uninsured residents of Los Angeles County, I volunteered in a primary medical care clinic in a low-income Hispanic community. The physician, nursing, and administrative staff of the clinic welcomed me and appreciated my donation of services. Medical staff consisted largely of family practice residents supervised by a faculty attending.

There were a variety of reimbursement programs, depending on whether the patient required a mammogram, obstetrical care, or had more complex problems. Reimbursement for almost all of the patients that I saw came from the LAC-DHS through the "Public Private Partnership" (PPP). This PPP program was part of the LAC-DHS reengineering strategy designed to increase the primary care services to LA County uninsured residents. Before 1995, all the LAC-DHS funding for medical care for the medically uninsured residents was channeled through the public hospitals and clinics.

70

In the first two half-day clinic sessions, I saw only about 10 patients. Only one was new to the clinic and required an initial evaluation. The others all came each month for refills of their medications for diabetes, high blood pressure, hypercholesterolemia, arthritis, and menopause. The PPP program administrators apparently reimbursed the contracting clinics according to the number of patient visits. The clinic visit fee included the cost of medications, so this encouraged the contracted providers to have patients return for frequent visits rather than providing medication refills that would have reduced the net reimbursement.

So much for the financial advantages of outsourcing the care of the poor from LAC-DHS clinics to private ones.

Chapter 9

The Civil Service Hearing

On April 27, 1999, the long-awaited civil service hearing began, pitting David K. Cundiff, MD against the County of Los Angeles. In an unusual move, LA County management hired a private attorney, Lucian Schmit, Esq., rather than using the County-employed legal staff. I retained Larry Rosenzweig, Esq., an attorney recommended to me by Joe Bader, the representative for the Union of American Physicians and Dentists, the union vying to represent County physicians in bargaining with management. The hearing officer designated by the LA County Civil Service Commission was Shelly Kaufman, Esq., a private attorney who was highly regarded by Mr. Rosenzweig.

About five days before the hearing, the attorneys exchanged documents that would be entered into evidence. This was the first time the County representatives had a chance to see my defense. A hospital peer-review committee had considered my thrombosis case (Item #1, page. 52-53) and convicted me of substandard care without allowing me to present a defense. This violated both state law and the hospital bylaws.

David Goldstein, MD's Testimony

Management called David Goldstein, MD as the first witness for the prosecution. He reviewed the thrombosis case and recounted his 15-minute interview of me regarding it. He said that I demonstrated to him that I didn't know that the popliteal vein was a deep proximal leg vein. They submitted as exhibits four drawings from an anatomy atlas that highlighted where the popliteal vein is in the leg. They also entered into evidence the Doppler ultrasound study of the thrombosed popliteal vein of my patient. I didn't contest any of these anatomical points.

Later, he indicated that he had read the exhibit summarizing my defense and acknowledged that my concern about the patient bleeding with Coumadin might have been valid. However, Dr. Goldstein said that, if I stopped the Coumadin, I should have sent the patient to have a blood filter (i.e., Greenfield Filter) inserted through the patient's groin into his inferior vena cava, the largest vein in the lower half of the body. On cross examination, my attorney asked him if any controlled studies in the literature proved that inserting a Greenfield Filter reduced the chance of dying in patients with DVTs. He answered truthfully, "No."

Attorney Lucian Schmit led Dr. Goldstein through the introduction into evidence of the other six charges. Dr. Goldstein said little to justify each of the charges as a cause supporting termination. When asked what other clinical errors I had made, he mentioned my prescribing a totally plant-based diet (i.e., vegan diet) for an obese type 2 diabetic patient. (Appendix #205) I detailed the medical reasoning for my action in a grievance proceeding (Appendix #203), but it was denied. Dr. Goldstein ordered me to take remedial training on the nutritional aspects of diabetes mellitus. (Appendix #199)

He also commented on a patient with a broken leg and a lung mass in which I decided to have the leg fixed before having the lung mass evaluated. (Appendices #200 and #206) LAC+USC Medical Center grievance officer Dr. Albert Yellin denied my defense of my management of the case (Appendix #203 – Case 2) and Dr. Goldstein ordered me to take remedial education in reading chest x-rays. (Appendix #199)

In this series of my cases that he alleged were below the standard of medical care, Dr. Goldstein next mentioned a patient that I referred to quality assurance who suffered severe pain needlessly at home for months before being admitted to my service while actively dying of cancer. The following was my letter to LAC-USC Medical Center Medical Director Dr. Ronald Kauffman and the QA Committee:

> On April 4, 1996, Mrs. DD, an elderly woman, was admitted to my internal medicine service in extreme pain and was actively dying. My residents quickly surmised that the patient had been followed by the LAC+USC Medical Oncology service for widely metastatic malignancy. The medical records did not show that Mrs. DD had an advanced directive or whether or not she should be resuscitated when the complications of the cancer stopped her heart.

Fortunately, we found Mrs. DD's sister-in-law and confirmed a "do not resuscitate status." We controlled her severe pain with IV morphine. She died within hours.

In the letter, I suggested that Dr. Kaufman call the daughter to explain why her mother had to suffer so much pain in her last few weeks of life. Dr. Kaufman called the daughter and subsequently wrote the following in a letter to me about their conversation: (Appendix #151)

> In your memo of April 4, 1996, you suggested that I call Doris, the sister-in-law of one of the patients you summarize. I promptly followed your suggestion. She was pleased to be offered an opportunity to express her views regarding the care at the Medical Center. She was highly complementary of Dr. Vukasin from the Colorectal Service. She was especially grateful for the bedside manner, concern and communication that he provided. She was complimentary of the hospital care she received. However, she expressed concern about the large numbers of patients that are scheduled for the outpatient clinics and the long waits that are required.

> Doris expressed concern as to why you never returned her calls in early February. Since the time in October 1995, when you represented yourself as her oncologist, they looked to you for help with pain problems. I intend to get more details about this interaction; however, it is my understanding that this is not your present assignment. Additionally, by interposing yourself on this clinical situation you set up the situation which you are so concerned about. Doris' call to the oncology service was made specifically to you, because you were clear in having them call you for any problems. In doing this you misrepresented your role in this case. Finally, in reviewing the final admission medical record, I do not find any evidence that you

participated in the care of this case. This is
inconsistent with your Department's policy.

By copy of this memo, I am requesting that the
Department of Medicine evaluate your role in this case
and the expectations that you created in this family.

My response to Dr. Kaufman indicated that he had confused me
with the patient's medical oncology fellow: (Appendix #152)

In your memo of 4/5/96 concerning the absence of
opioids for cancer pain prior to about eight hours
before her death, you said that I was managing the
patient's pain since October 1995. In fact, I have not
been involved with the Pain and Palliative Care
Service since September 15, 1995 and never saw Mrs.
DD. until about 12:00 pm 4/4/96 when she was
actively dying. Perhaps your confusion is due to the
similarity between my name, Cundiff, and the medical
oncology fellow who followed Mrs. DD, Dr. Bhrama
Konda.

Concerning the documentation of my participation in
the care of Mrs. DD, during her final hospital
admission on my service, my signature appears on the
order to "continue current care but no resuscitation."
My Cardinal Red team was engaged in attending
rounds when we heard of an unstable cancer patient
admitted to our team. After rounds at about 12:00
PM, we went to ward 1200 (admitting area) to see her.
Fortunately, Ms. Y., the sister-in-law, arrived and I
was able to discuss the patient's prognosis and get her
concordance with the DNR plan. At that time the
intern's and resident's H & P (histories and physicals)
were not available to countersign and I was late for
my El Monte CHC clinic which begins at 1 PM. By the
time that I returned to the hospital after clinic, Mrs.
DD had died. I looked for the chart on 6300 to co-sign

the notes of the houseofficers, but the chart had
already been taken to the morgue.

I hope this clarifies my role in this case.

After my letter to clear up Dr. Kaufman's confusion about last
names, I received no verbal or written apology and no further
attention was given to the case. He would have been happy to
discipline me in this case, if I had not returned the family's desperate
calls for help. However, he did not pursue the matter when he found
that the Medical Oncology staff let the patient suffer at home for
weeks with no recourse other than to come to the emergency room for
admission to the hospital.

Dr. Goldstein next testified that I was insubordinate in asking to
be excused from additional attending duties due to my weight-bearing
hip pain. (Appendices #136, #137, #138, #139, and #141) He testified
that he didn't think that I was malingering. He didn't explain why he
left this as a charge supporting my termination after I did the
assignments that he ordered me to do.

None of these six other charges used to support my termination
from the LAC-DHS could be characterized as malpractice. For
malpractice to occur there has to be a clinical error in judgment or
technique and the error needs to have caused harm to a patient. The
patient who died of lung clots after I discontinued the Coumadin
certainly suffered harm. However, the issue of whether it was
malpractice on my part depended on whether the medical community
considered it reasonable to stop an anticoagulant in a patient at high
risk for bleeding.

In the next part of his testimony, Dr. Goldstein enumerated the
following complaints that he had with my directorship of the Cancer
and AIDS Pain Service:

- Direct care was provided to patients without teaching the
  interns and residents to properly treat pain.
- Only 50 internal medicine residents served on rotations on the
  Cancer and AIDS Pain Service.
- Other clinical services like neurology, anesthesiology, and
  psychiatry were not brought in to the Cancer and AIDS Pain
  Service.

These issues were not unique to the LAC+USC Cancer and AIDS Pain Service. In my view, they reflected a lack of understanding on his part of the obstacles to good palliative care.

My attorney asked Dr. Goldstein if he had read my op-ed article in the *LA Times* regarding the hospital replacement project. (Appendix #194) After a long pause, Dr. Goldstein admitted that he had read it and agreed with some of the points in the article and disagreed with others. He implied that it had no significant impact on LAC-DHS policymakers and denied that this played any role in my termination from County service.

Agueta Hurst, Pharm D's Testimony

The senior pharmacist on the Anticoagulation Service, Agueta Hurst, Pharm D., testified next about her role in the thrombosis case. She did not actually see the patient, but supervised the pharmacist who consulted on the patient. She described herself as the "drug lady" and lamented that, at the time of this case, no hematologist was assigned to head the service. The previous hematologist director of the Anticoagulation Service had retired.

Dr. Hurst testified that having a popliteal DVT is an indication for Coumadin. She stated that she had recommended that I continue the Coumadin anticoagulant in the patient with the popliteal DVT.

On cross-examination, my attorney asked Dr. Hurst to estimate the incidence of DVT per year in the United States. She had no idea. He followed by quizzing her on the risk of bleeding to death with a course of Coumadin for DVT. She couldn't even hazard a guess. Finally, he asked her whether she had recommended the placement of a Greenfield Filter in the patient since I had stopped the Coumadin. She responded that she wasn't a doctor and, therefore, not clinically qualified to make such a recommendation. Dr. Hurst again complained about the fact that no hematologist was on the Anticoagulation Service at the time. She probably did not know that I am a board certified hematologist.

In my view, Mr. Rosenzweig, my attorney, had skillfully shown that the Anticoagulation Service could monitor the drugs, but not be trusted with clinical decisions involving the risks and benefits of treatment.

Ewa Konca, MD, Intern on the Service

Lucian Schmit next called Ewa Konca, MD, one of the interns on my service during the month that the DVT patient died. She emigrated from Poland where she was an excellent scholar and athlete. At her peak as a sprinter in track, she was among the 20 fastest women runners in the world.

I don't know why the prosecution called her. Since Dr. Konca was not the intern assigned to the patient, she could only report hearsay accounts of what the other intern told her that he heard from the radiologist.

As the first question on cross-examination, Mr. Rosenzweig asked her if I was a good teacher. She said yes and then spoke at length about how I always answered my pages and made myself available to help the team with difficult clinical problems. She went on to report that she learned a great deal from my clinical perspective, particularly on pain management and palliative care. Dr. Konca spoke so passionately that both my attorney and I thought that she might begin crying before she completed her statement.

Lucian Schmit was visibly shaken by this powerful testimonial of his witness on my behalf.

Malini Shah, MD, Senior Resident on the Service

The senior resident on my team in the fateful month, Malini Shah, MD, took the stand after some inconsequential testimony by David Zamorano, the LAC-DHS personnel officer. Dr. Shah came from India and was in a combined internal medicine and pediatrics residency. I appreciated having her teaching, directing, and supervising the other residents.

On questioning by Mr. Schmit, Dr. Shaw reaffirmed that the ultimate decision about whether to continue or stop the anticoagulation was mine. She followed my order to stop Coumadin.

Mr. Rosenzweig opened the cross-examination by asking if I was a good teacher. She said, "Excellent." He followed by asking if the one-month rotation on my service had favorably influenced her clinical practice subsequently. She said, "Very favorably."

Albert Yellin, MD, Chief of Vascular Surgery

The County's witness list given to my attorney included Howard Leibman, MD of the LAC+USC Medical Center Hematology Department. We expected that his job would be to say that my stopping the anticoagulation was below the community standard. Having a hematologist and anticoagulation specialist testify against me should have been an essential part of the County's case against me.

Both my attorney and I were surprised when they called Albert Yellin, MD, the Chief of Vascular Surgery at LAC+USC Medical Center in lieu of Dr. Leibman. Perhaps Dr. Leibman was out of town or unavailable. More likely, he had read my response to the charges of the County and didn't want to tarnish his reputation by saying that my care was substandard.

Dr. Yellin's entire medical career of over 30 years had been at USC. He had been the hearing officer to hear the last two of my grievances. Hearing officer Shelly Kaufman overruled Mr. Rosenzweig's objection that Dr. Yellin's previous role as my grievance hearing officer made him biased against me.

It seemed to be a strategic error on the part of the County to use a surgeon as the only authority on anticoagulation therapy of DVT. Generally, and at LAC+USC Medical Center, hematologists run the anticoagulation services. Twenty-five or 30 years ago, it was common for surgeons to operate on the thrombosed veins in the thigh as a treatment of DVT. However, this treatment led to increased risk of morbidity and mortality and has been discredited. The primary experience of surgeons in the thromboembolism field is with trying to prevent DVTs after operations.

Dr. Yellin said that the patient with the DVT could have had his Coumadin therapy carefully monitored in a nursing home, or a visiting nurse might have been sent to his home to draw his blood periodically for monitoring. This had never been mentioned by anyone before, and I wondered why he was bringing it up now. I didn't figure out why he testified this way until the Medical Board hearing about a year later.

Dr. Yellin called my decision to stop the Coumadin clearly below the standard of care in the community. Appearing to hedge his bets, he said that if I thought that three months of outpatient Coumadin therapy in this man was too risky, then I should have had the radiologist place an inferior vena cava filter (i.e., Greenfield Filter).

On cross-examination, Mr. Rosenzweig first asked about the risks of placing an inferior vena cava filter and leaving it in place for life. Dr. Yellin acknowledged some occasional serious problems, but would not give a specific estimate of the risk of morbidity and mortality from the procedure in a sick population of patients. My attorney next asked if any controlled studies in the literature showed that the Greenfield Filter reduced mortality of DVT. Dr. Yellin said that no such studies existed because it would take 100,000 patients in a study to give a statistically positive result.

This statement put the County in the position of now asserting that I was below the standard of care because I didn't order the Greenfield Filter. No mention of the Greenfield Filter was made by the Anticoagulation Service or in the letter terminating me from the County. Additionally, Dr. Yellin put the County in the position of maintaining that a potentially risky and scientifically unproven therapy was the standard of care.

I was pleased. I thought that no judge would convict me on the basis of Dr. Yellin's testimony.

No "Decision Maker" Testimony

The County attorney wanted to follow the usual protocol for an appeal of a dismissal and call a "decision-maker," such as Ronald Kaufman, MD, Medical Director of LAC+USC Medical Center or Donald Thomas, MD, Medical Director of the LAC-DHS. However, no one of the higher-ranking administrators was available, so the County forfeited the opportunity. I suspect that they may have feared answering questions on cross-examination regarding the effects on their decision of my *LA Times* op-ed article (Exhibit 6) and my letters to Quality Assurance about poor pain treatment. We were also prepared to ask the decision-maker if they knew of my claim to Medicaid administrators that the LAC+USC Medical Center defrauded Medicaid out of over $200 million per year (Chapter 6). Their sworn testimony about high-level discussions on this issue would have been interesting.

Matthew Conolly, MD, Expert Witness for the Defense

On the second day of the hearing, my attorney called Matthew Conolly, MD a professor of medicine from UCLA as my only expert witness. Dr. Conolly started a cancer pain service at UCLA at about the same time that I started mine at LAC+USC. On one occasion, in the early 1990s, he came to LAC+USC for an afternoon of seeing patients with me. We had occasionally seen each other in meetings of pain specialists. I found out on the day of his testimony that he was from Epsom, England, the place I married my wife 30 years before.

The report by Shelley Kaufman, Hearing Officer of the Civil Service Commission, included the following:

> Dr. Conolly specializes in internal medicine. He is employed by the UCLA Medical Center. He reviewed the chart of Patient BR and the report written by Dr. Cundiff. He concluded that given the clinical setting it was appropriate to cease the anticoagulant therapy. These factors included that the patient was homeless; he had no money for medical care; he had open tuberculosis, demonstrating extensive lung disease; he was anemic, which is a contraindication to anticoagulation therapy; and he was alcoholic with liver disease, which can have a negative effect on the anticoagulation medicine.

Prosecutor Schmit on cross-examination asked Dr. Conolly if I had addressed the possibility of ordering a Greenfield Filter. Dr. Conolly referred to the section of my written response to the charges that quoted the guidelines from the Fourth American College of Chest Physicians Consensus Conference on Antithrombotic Therapy. He emphasized that inserting the filter has risks and has not been proven to reduce mortality.

Out of the goodness of his heart, Dr. Conolly charged me nothing for his time preparing or testifying.

I was feeling better all the time about the progress of this trial.

David K. Cundiff, MD, the Appellant's Testimony

Mr. Rosenzweig called me as the last witness for the defense. I chronicled my 19-year career in the LAC-DHS, beginning in the Medical Oncology Section at Harbor-UCLA Medical Center and emphasizing my three-year stint in the Hematology Section at LAC+USC in the early 1980s. I also described my years as director of the Cancer and AIDS Pain Service and the three years doing general medical attending after the Service closed.

I detailed my analysis in the case at hand, stating that I thought outpatient Coumadin was too risky for medical, social, and institutional reasons. I addressed the Greenfield Filter issue by referring to the medical literature's lack of proof that it reduces mortality of DVT. My attorney and I marched through most of the other six charges supporting my termination with my side of the story.

I also spoke about several points raised by the prosecution. One important rebuttal point involved Dr. Yellin's contention that the patient with the DVT could have had his Coumadin therapy carefully monitored in a nursing home or a visiting nurse might have drawn his blood periodically for monitoring. I said that Medi-Cal would not pay for nursing home placement just to monitor the anticoagulant. Even if Medi-Cal would pay, the patient wouldn't have agreed to nursing home placement. Concerning the possibility of visiting nurses drawing the blood for Coumadin monitoring, I stated that I had never seen that occur in my 19-years of County service. If that was possible, all patients on Coumadin anticoagulation would want that service instead of spending days in the clinic.

Mr. Schmit's cross-examination questions appeared to do me no perceptible damage and seemed to have helped my case further. He made the point that since 1984 I wasn't certified by the hospital to practice hematology. This only seemed to emphasize the point that I was a board-certified hematologist and the County had not brought a hematologist as an expert witness.

Mr. Schmit referred to a letter by Dr. Michael Patzakis, Chief of Orthopedic Surgery, responding to my charge that he undertreated a patient's pain. (Appendices #207, #209, and #211) He called me to explain why Dr. Patzakis called me "a danger to patients." I explained that I wrote the letter to Quality Assurance after Dr.

Patzakis refused to address my concern about a patient's pain. It was not my behavior in the interaction or my concern about a patient's pain that he called unprofessional conduct. Dr. Patzakis said it was unprofessional of me to write up the incident as a referral to Quality Assurance with a copy to the chief of the LAC-DHS. As detailed in my letter to Dr. Kaufman and the QA Committee, I wrote the letter of concern only after my discussion with Drs. Patzakis and Holtom failed to get them to increase the patient's pain medications.

Mr. Schmit next questioned me about my 83 cases referred to the Quality Assurance Committee. He asked me how many letters I had written to the Quality Assurance Committee before leaving the Service. I responded that it was between two and four. He questioned why the sudden increase in late 1995. I said that while physicians all over the Medical Center were consulting me to help them manage pain in their most difficult patients, I had no reason to alienate them by writing letters to Quality Assurance. After the closure of the Service, I saw it as a constructive way of continuing to advocate for better pain control even though Dr. Ronald Kaufman, LAC+USC Medical Director, had asked me to stop on several occasions.

Mr. Schmit asked if my letters were in retaliation for being fired from the Service. I replied to the effect that it wasn't out of vindictiveness toward the administration, but rather out of concern for the patients. I said that I enjoyed my ward and clinic medical attending job even more than the Pain and Palliative Care Service because I could be the primary care doctor rather than the consultant. It also gave me more opportunity to teach general internal medicine to the housestaff and medical students and to learn from them.

After I completed my testimony, Mr. Schmit waived the opportunity to call rebuttal witnesses and rested its case. We also rested our case. My attorney and I were very pleased with the hearing. The attorneys submitted their written closing briefs on May 12, 1999. (Appendices #321 and #322)

Hearing Officer Shelly Kaufman's Decision

The ruling by Shelly Kaufman in my LA County Civil Service Hearing concluded as follows:

84

The Civil Service Hearing

Findings of Fact

1. At all times material herein, Appellant was employed by Respondent as a physician specialist with the Los Angeles County Department of Health Services.
2. On February 7, 1998, patient BR was transferred from Pomona Valley Hospital to LAC-USC with a diagnosis of tuberculosis and deep vein thrombosis in the popliteal vein. The patient was receiving intravenous and oral anticoagulants.
3. The popliteal vein is a vein in the leg posterior to the knee continuing on into the upper leg posterior to and rather near the femur.
4. The most significant danger posed by a deep vein thrombosis is the risk that the clot will dislodge and travel to the heart or lungs.
5. Patient BR was under the care of Dr. Cundiff and his medicine team.
6. On February 11, 1998, Dr. Cundiff ordered discontinuance of the anticoagulant medications provided to Patient BR.
7. The patient died on February 19, 1998 due to a pulmonary embolism.
8. Dr. Cundiff did not discuss with Patient BR the risk factors of discontinuing the anticoagulants or the obligations involved if oral anticoagulation therapy is continued.
9. Dr. Cundiff's decision to discontinue the anticoagulant treatment fell below the standard of care.

Conclusions of Law

1. Respondent has met its burden of proof that the allegations set forth in the letter of discharge dated October 15, 1998 are true.
2. Respondent has met its burden of proof that discharge is the appropriate remedy.

Recommendation

It is respectfully submitted that the discharge be sustained.

Chapter 10

Medical Board Hearing

Since I was terminated from my position at LAC-USC Medical Center because of medical malpractice or other inappropriate behavior, Dr. Ronald Kaufman was required to report the reasons for the termination to the California Medical Board. In his report to the Board, he described the action against me as follows:

> A series of personnel issues resulted in Dr. Cundiff's termination. This termination was in accordance with the Los Angeles County Department of Health Services document "The Discipline Guidelines for Licensed Medical Professionals (Section 7000)." There were five instances of written warnings for failure to comply with supervisory instructions. There was a single instance of unprofessional conduct evidenced by failure to work with other physicians in a collaborative manner. Another issue was a therapeutic failure in the care of a patient who was hospitalized for deep venous thrombosis and died during the episode of care. A panel of peer physicians who found the care to be below the applicable professional and community standard reviewed the error in the care of this patient.

To investigate the charges that LAC-DHS used to terminate my employment, the California Medical Board assigned Kathleen Schmidt, Supervising Investigator, Shirley Russo, Senior Investigator, and H. D. Mosier, MD, Medical Consultant. (Appendix #343) The pertinent sections of the initial memorandum from Dr. Mosier to the two investigators (Appendix #344) was as follows:

ALLEGED VIOLATIONS

BUSINESS AND PROFESSIONS CODE SECTION 2234 (b) – Gross Negligence

BUSINESS AND PROFESSIONS CODE SECTION 2234 (c) –
Repeated Negligent Acts
BUSINESS AND PROFESSIONS CODE SECTION 2234 (d) –
Incompetence

MEDICAL CONSULTANT'S COMMENTS

It is apparent from the documents supplied by Dr. Cundiff that his review by peer committees at LAC/USC covered other patients than just the patient with the deep vein thrombosis. While his performance in other cases was considered below par, the County has elected to state in the 805 report that Dr. Cundiff's dismissal was based on a review of one case of deep vein thrombosis and a single incidence of unprofessional conduct evidenced "by failure to work with other physicians in a collaborative manner." Dr. Cundiff's alleged failure to work collaboratively is not clearly covered by documents supplied by Dr. Kaufman. Based on documents supplied by LAC/USC, it would appear that Dr. Cundiff was dismissed on the basis of bad judgment in one medical case, for which he has expressed sorrow, and for a long history of personnel problems. . . .

MEDICAL CONSULTANT'S CONCLUSIONS

Documentation supplied by LAC/USC Medical Center indicates that Dr. David K. Cundiff was terminated from his permanent position in the LA County system on the basis of a wrong decision in one case of deep vein thrombosis and his failure to work collaboratively with other physicians. The supporting documents leave the latter matter unclear. . . .

Complaint to California Medical Board about LAC+USC Medical Director Ronald Kaufman, MD

While the Medical Board was investigating a formal complaint from Dr. Kaufman about me, I lodged a formal complaint that he failed to investigate and report the results of the 83 referrals that I sent to the Quality Assurance Committee about poor pain management. In two letters to the Board, I documented how my termination was in retaliation for my activism about improving pain control at the hospital.

> Letter #1 (Appendix #342)
> February 11, 1999
> Dear Complaints Investigator,
>
> I wish to register a complaint against Ronald Kaufman, MD, Medical Director of LA County+USC Medical Center. In September 1995, Dr. Kaufman authorized the closure of the Pain and Palliative Care Service at the LAC+USC Medical Center. When Supervisor Michael Antonovich inquired about this at my urging, he was told, "The Department of Health Services has indicated that LAC+USC Medical Center will have available staff to consult regarding difficult cases and ongoing education of residents and staff regarding pain control." Dr. Kaufman also gave assurances that "LAC+USC will monitor the adequacy of the pain control program through its quality assurance process and will take appropriate actions to modify the program as necessary within available resources. . . ." (Appendix #150)
>
> Letter #2 (Appendix #353)
> February 1999
> Re: Complaint against Ronald Kaufman, MD
>
> Dear Consumer Complaint Manager,
>
> Enclosed are letters of concern about the management of 83 patients at the LA County+USC Medical Center over the years 1994 to 1998. The Quality Assurance Committee did not send me any reports of investigations concerning these letters. The only written response that I received was in the form of the minutes to a special meeting of the Quality Assurance Committee. (Appendix #154) These minutes reflect that LAC-USC administrators asked me to stop

writing letters of concern about undertreatment of pain.

I expressed my concern to Mark Finucane, Director of LAC-DHS, and requested that my referral letters to Quality Assurance be sent to an outside group for evaluation (Appendix #323). He did not respond. . . .

Letter #3 (Appendix #356)
June 23, 1999
Dear Consumer Complaint Manager,

I am writing to send additional documents regarding three of the patients that I referred to your office last month. In all three cases, I wrote prescriptions for opioid medications for treatment of chronic pain after the patients could not get their medications from other LAC+USC physicians. As a result of my writing these prescriptions, I received the letter dated October 14, 1998 (attached) from my supervisor, David Goldstein, MD. . . .

Meeting with California Medical Board Investigators

I met with David Mosier, MD, regional chief, and Kathy Schmidt, administrator, of the Medical Board of California in mid-February 1999. I had prepared them by sending an earlier draft of this book. Our 3-1/2 hour meeting covered my history in the profession of medicine from medical school to my termination by the LAC-DHS. They appeared sympathetic to my cause.

Ms. Schmidt brought up the case that had recently aired on the *20/20* television show about the physician accused of undertreating the pain of a terminal cancer patient (see Chapter 8, "Doctor Sued for Undertreating Cancer Pain").[1] I told them that I had documented 83 such cases at the LAC-USC Medical Center and that I was considering referring them to the Medical Board of California. They said that, to their knowledge, the Medical Board of California had disciplined no physician for the undertreatment of pain. However, they invited me to send them in and promised that each one would be thoroughly investigated.

I did report the cases to the California Medical Board and they were not investigated.

Dr. Mosier said that they would be sending my DVT case out for review by an expert in that field. I asked if they would also investigate the other two cases in which LAC-USC peer review committees found my treatment decisions substandard but did not report to the Board. I told them that this pattern of harassment of me for apparently political reasons warranted a more in-depth investigation. They were not enthusiastic about widening their required investigation, but deferred the final decision to their legal council.

At the end of the meeting Kathy Schmidt said that they hoped to have a favorable ruling for me in time for the civil service hearing.

The relevant sections of Dr. Mosier's memorandum (Appendix #345) regarding the meeting with me are as follows:

MEDICAL CONSULTANT'S COMMENTS

The difficulty that Dr. Cundiff had with LAC/USC Medical Center appears to have stemmed largely because of his failure to fit easily into the bureaucratic framework. It is clear that Dr. Cundiff has strong feelings with regard to patient care, and that he feels compelled to point out problems when he sees them. This has led to his circulation of complaints, both within and outside of the LAC/USC system regarding patient care. The file shows that Dr. Cundiff has been politically active in combating some of the plans for expansion at USC. Dr. Cundiff has done this because he is convinced that patient care will suffer if these plans materialize.

The 805 Report lists other problems involving failures to work well with other physicians or to collaborate well with them. However, the review of this file by the Medical Board focuses on the quality of care issue in the case of BR. The file will go out for review by an expert in medical hematology. That review will be limited to the issues in the BR case, particularly with regard to Dr. Cundiff's decision to discontinue anticoagulation therapy.

MEDICAL CONSULTANT'S RECOMMENDATIONS

I recommend that this file go to an expert in medical hematology or hematology/oncology for a review of the quality of care rendered by Dr. Cundiff and his team to patient BR. The principle problem to be addressed in the review is the decision to discontinue anticoagulation therapy.

Report of the Hematology "Expert"

R.S. Vasan, MD reviewed my case for the Medical Board as the expert in hematology. While I am Board certified in internal medicine, medical oncology (cancer), and hematology (blood), Dr. Vasan is only certified in internal medicine and medical oncology— not hematology. The relevant sections of Dr. Vasan's report (Appendix #346) are as follows:

STANDARD OF PRACTICE

A reasonable standard of practice for an internist in approaching a 59-year-old male admitted with a diagnosis of tuberculosis, malnutrition, and deep vein thrombosis would involve starting the patient immediately on intravenous anticoagulants and follow up with oral anticoagulants. The usual intravenous anticoagulant that is used is Heparin. . . . Following initial heparinization, the patient is usually started on Coumadin. . . . The Coumadin is then continued at least for six weeks in most situations. The standard of practice usually involves Coumadinization for a three-month period. . . .

DEPARTURES/VIOLATIONS FROM STANDARD OF PRACTICE

Mr. BR, a 59-year-old gentleman, the patient in question, was started on Heparin and Coumadin on the day of admission on February 7, 1998. On February 11, 1998, the medical team caring for the patient under the direction of Dr. Cundiff was told by Dr. Cundiff to stop anticoagulation.

The reasons, according to Dr. Cundiff, were:

The patient was an indigent and cannot be relied upon to follow-up regularly in an outpatient clinic to monitor anticoagulation therapy with Coumadin.

NOTE: *Even if Dr. Cundiff thought that the patient may not be a candidate for outpatient Coumadinization, the patient should have continued anticoagulation at least for the length of time that he was in the hospital. Considering the fact that his sputum for AFB (tuberculosis) continued to be positive, he was not a candidate for discharge very soon. Be that as it may, the anticoagulation was stopped in four days, which is clearly not adequate when the literature suggests unequivocally that anticoagulation for deep vein thrombosis should continue at least for six weeks.*

In his interview with Dr. Mosier, Dr. Cundiff states that the literature is not clear about the treatment of popliteal vein thrombosis. He questions whether the popliteal vein is a deep vein.

NOTE: *Be it anatomical location the popliteal vein should be considered a deep vein and not otherwise.*

It is therefore my opinion that the medical care rendered to Mr. BR was an extreme departure from accepted standards of medical practice.

93

Based on documents supplied by Dr. Kaufman and the opinion of Dr. Vasan, Dr. Mosier and his team decided to proceed with an accusation against me. (Appendix #331) Because of the way the case developed, it is notable that the accusation stated that the patient was homeless. It did not challenge the documentation in the chart that the patient was alcoholic. The Board followed the accusation with a request for discovery, including information about a stipulated settlement. (Appendix #341)

Amazing Discovery: Alcoholism is a Contraindication for Coumadin!

At the Civil Service Hearing appealing my termination of employment with LAC-DHS, my principle defense of stopping the Coumadin was that it was a judgment call in a patient that could have died of clots in his lungs or from bleeding from Coumadin. My expert witness, Dr. Conolly, defended my decision and Dr. Yellin called it malpractice. The lay judge had to decide which of these two medical experts to believe. After Judge Kauffman chose to discount my witness and believe Dr. Yellin, I searched for more compelling evidence to support my case in preparation for the Medical Board hearing.

While researching medical literature, I carefully read the *Physician's Desk Reference* documentation about Coumadin. The same detailed chemical and clinical information about any drug in the PDR is also dispensed with each bottle of medication as the package insert. In the "contraindications" section concerning Coumadin, it included "alcoholism."

The patient's chart recorded that he admitted to drinking a six-pack of beer per day for 20 years before quitting six months previously. My medical resident recorded in the chart that he was alcoholic. At the LA County Civil Service Hearing, I mentioned that my judgment to stop the Coumadin was based on the patient's liver failure, anemia, difficulty in coming to clinics for anticoagulant monitoring, and his alcoholism. The prosecution did not challenge the alcoholism diagnosis written in the chart.

If a physician prescribes a drug that is contraindicated for a patient's condition and an adverse event occurs, the doctor is guilty of malpractice—period. If I had continued the Coumadin and the patient had bled to death or had a disabling hemorrhagic stroke, I would have had absolutely no defense against a malpractice charge. I thought that this would stop the Medical Board in its tracks from prosecuting me.

Pre-Hearing Conference

In March 2000, at a conference preceding the scheduled hearing in front of Judge Navarette, I mentioned to Robert McKim Bell, Deputy Attorney General and Medical Board prosecuting attorney, that alcoholism is a contraindication to using Coumadin according to the PDR. Mr. Bell asked, "How do we know that the patient was alcoholic?" I said that in the Civil Service Hearing no one disputed that the patient was alcoholic. He then responded to preliminary hearing Judge Navarette that the rules in the Medical Board disciplinary hearings do not allow evidence to come from the *Physician's Desk Reference* or package inserts, only from testimony of experts. The reason was that dueling expert witnesses could confuse lay judges by entering lots of highly technical scientific articles from the medical literature. However, in their testimonies, medical experts can refer to information in the medical literature.

It surprised me that, on finding that I had a rock solid defense, the prosecution did not immediately fold.

Judge Navarette also denied my request to submit the results of the survey of 101 internists and anticoagulation researchers about the best treatment of the patient's DVT and the treatment options that would be considered malpractice. My expert witness, Matthew Conolly, MD, and I conducted this survey after the Civil Service Hearing (TheHealthEconomy.com/ChaptersMDM.pdf pages 407–418). Mr. Bell argued that the survey was "hearsay" and submitted 16 pages of published legal cases about the issue of entering surveys into the legal record. The Judge sustained Mr. Bell's objection. Regarding the critical issue of whether stopping the Coumadin was or was not below the standard of care, my fate in the Medical Board Hearing would depend on whether the new judge would believe Dr. Conolly, my expert witness, or Albert Yellin, MD, the County's expert witness.

Mr. Bell tried very hard to get me to settle the case. If I admitted that my decision to stop the Coumadin constituted malpractice, he was prepared to offer me probation that would allow me to continue practicing medicine with some restrictions. I would also have had to do some remedial studies in proper prescribing in the area of anticoagulation medicine.

I refused to settle.

The Medical Board Hearing

On May 8, 2000, the hearing for my license to practice medicine in the State of California began. (Appendices #347, #348, #349, #350, and #351) Stewart Waxman, an Administrative Law Judge, presided. Mr. Bell first called Shirley Russo (Appendix #347, pgs. 23 -38), Medical Board Investigator, to the stand. In the following excerpt, Ms. Russo testified that, when she interviewed me about the case, I said that the patient's alcoholism was one reason that persuaded me to stop the Coumadin:

> Q. And did alcoholism come up in the course of the discussion?
> A. Yes.
> Q. In what context?
> A. According to Dr. Cundiff, Mr. BR was an alcoholic.
> Q. And what consequence, if any, did that have on the decision to discontinue [the Coumadin]?
> A. Also that he may not be reliable and that he should not continue on his medication.
> Q. Did you accept both of those as factually true?
> A. Yes, we did.
> Q. And nobody challenged him on that?
> A. No, we didn't.
> Q. Did there later come a point in time when you were asked to look into the question of homelessness, residence and status, employment, and alcoholism of Mr. BR?
> A. Yes.
> Q. How did that come about?
> A. I was requested by Deputy Attorney Bell.
> Q. About how long ago?
> A. Six to eight weeks ago.

Ms. Russo went on to testify that, when she investigated Mr. BR's social situation at the request of Mr. Bell, she found some things that contradicted information in the medical chart. The patient was not homeless and had lived in the same apartment for 11 years. He was not unemployed and worked in a fast food restaurant. She also found that the patient's daughter Benita Poole disputed our diagnosis of alcoholism.

Ms. Poole did not testify in the Civil Service Commission appeal hearing (May 1999). Before Ms. Russo knocked on her door in late March or early April 2000, the LAC-DHS had not contacted Ms. Poole to inform her that I had been fired over my decision to stop Coumadin in her father's case. Undoubtedly, they knew that to inform her that a serious error had occurred in her father's care would have assured an expensive malpractice suit.

Obviously, after the pre-hearing in March when I broadcast that I was using the defense that Coumadin is contraindicated in alcoholics, Mr. Bell set about finding a counter argument. From February 1998, when the patient died, until March 2000, prosecutors did not challenge the well-documented diagnosis of alcoholism. For that matter, they did not dispute the record in the chart that he was homeless and unemployed.

LAC-DHS management had decided to risk Ms. Poole's malpractice suit in order to defeat me at the Medical Board Hearing.

Benita Poole, Patient's Daughter, Testifies

Next, the patient's daughter was sworn in, stating her occupation as "substance abuse counselor." She testified that her father lived in an apartment and worked as a chef at KFC Restaurant. When her father complained of pain in his leg, she brought him to Pomona Valley Hospital Emergency Room. She testified that she spoke with the reception clerk about social details for the chart record while the doctor questioned and examined her father. Regarding her father's use of alcohol, she answered Mr. Bell's questions (Appendix #347, pages 38– 58) as follows:

> Q. Now, the subject has come up whether your father
>   was an alcoholic or had alcohol liver disease. I'm

sure you couldn't look at his liver. Was your dad
an alcoholic as you knew?

A. No. Not to my knowledge, no.

Q. Did you have an opportunity to observe his
alcohol in a social setting?

A. Yes.

Q How would you characterize it?

A. Social.

Q. For example?

A. For example—let me see. He drank beer once in a
while. Those times—a couple of times whenever he
watched a game with my husband he just drank
beer. It was nothing I would think was a lot or
abusing.

Q. Okay. As a substance-abuse counselor, you think
you would have picked up on it if your father was
a drunk?

A. Yes.

Q. Had he ever been a drunk, to your knowledge?

A. Not to my knowledge.

Q. Did he (your father) ever, in your presence, tell
anyone falsely that he was an alcoholic or
homeless?

A. Not in my presence.

Q. So as you think of it, do you think it's likely that
your father could have given a phony story about
being homeless and an alcoholic and unemployed
to the people at the hospital where he was?

A. No.

On the last day of the hearing, Mr. Bell brought Ms. Poole back
as a rebuttal witness to further clarify her father's drinking history.
Ms. Poole disputed all of Dr. Karunananthan's facts about his
drinking. (Appendix #350, pages 114–118)

Q. MR. BELL: I'd like to clarify a couple of facts
which concerns your father's use of alcohol and
tobacco. And this question has been raised
through

the course of the trial. Were you at the time of his
death, in February of 1998, familiar as a matter of
personal observation over a span of years with
your
father's habits with respect to alcohol and
tobacco?

A. Yes.

Q. Then I think you testified you lived
within the same community in which your father
lived and met
with him at least once a week; is that correct?

A. Yes.

Q. Did your father have a preference in
what it is he drank in the way of alcoholic
beverages?

A. Yes.

Q. What was his preference?

A. Beer, malt liquor.

Q. The kind of beer we call malt liquor, which is
stronger than ordinary beer?

A. Yes.

Q. Did he have a favorite type or brand?

A. Yes, he did. I don't know the name. My husband
mentioned it.

Q. If I were to mention Colt 45, would that sound
right to you?

A. Yes.

Q. That's a malt beer, malt liquor beverage?

A. Yes.

Q. You saw your father drink this before; right?

A. Yes.

Q. When you saw him drink it, when would he be
drinking it? Was there a difference between
weekdays and weekends?

A. Yes.

Q. What was that difference?

A. The weekends, he drank the most.

Q. Would he drink during the week as a matter of
course?

A. I didn't see that. Maybe on one or two occasions during the week.

Q. All right.

A. And that would be in the evening, after work.

Q. And tell me about his weekend use of beer or malt liquor.

A. Of course, I talked to my husband to describe this to you guys.

Q. Just so long as you know what you're talking about.

A. Yes. The bottle my husband said is a quart, is what he used to drink, and he would drink on the weekends, and he would have no more than two of those for the weekend or for that day. He never finished two quarts a day.

Q. I see. And that was typical of your husband—your father? Your father would principally drink if he's going to drink on weekends; is that right?

A. Yes.

Q. When he would drink he would typically consume a malt liquor beverage called Colt 45?

A. Yes.

Q. He would purchase it not in the form of six packs but in individual bottles of approximately a quart in size?

A. Yes.

Q. And two bottles would do him for a day?

A. Yes.

Q. Did he often leave portions of his beer, as we'll call it for the people, unconsumed?

A. Yes.

Q. How would that happen?

A. Of course he's under the influence now. He will start talking and forget it was there and never finish it. And there was times on the weekend, whenever I would see him, he would have leftovers which I would know would be stale beer in his refrigerator that he never finished drinking.

Q. All right. Now, did he drink up until the time of
   his death?
A. Yes.
Q. I mean until he went to the hospital?
A. Yes.
Q. Did he quit drinking six months before that?
A. Not to my knowledge. No, he didn't.
Q. He didn't stop six months or any time before that?
A. No.

Mr. Bell did not dispute that alcoholism is a contraindication to the use of Coumadin. Despite his argument to Judge Navarette in the pretrial hearing that the defense couldn't use the package insert and the *Physician's Desk Reference* as evidence, he didn't question my right to refer to the PDR in court. He did not dispute that drinking a six-pack of beer per day for 20 years would warrant a diagnosis of alcoholism. Instead, he challenged the documentation in the chart about the amount of alcohol consumed and our diagnosis of alcoholism. (See testimony of medical resident Dr. Karunananthan to follow.)

After Ms. Poole testified that her father drank Colt 45 Malt Liquor and not cans of beer, I went directly to a liquor store and asked the attendant for a quart bottle of Colt 45. The attendant told me that there is no quart bottle of Colt 45; it only comes in 40-ounce magnums. I bought a magnum and found that it contains 6.25% alcohol versus 5% alcohol in beer. Consequently, two 40-ounce magnums have the alcohol equivalence of 8-1/2 12-ounce cans of beer.

I brought the magnum of Colt 45 to the courtroom the next day for the closing arguments and gave it to Mr. Rosenzweig. I asked him to show it to the judge in the closing argument and tell the judge how much alcohol it contains. Since a witness had not introduced this information into evidence, he told me that he could not show the bottle to the judge. I argued with him, but he was insistent. I thought that I would win anyway based on the new evidence that alcoholism is a contraindication to Coumadin use. However, I had also believed that I would win at the Civil Service Hearing, so I wanted to make sure.

Homelessness of Patient

There were four references to the patient's homelessness in the chart. After 48.5 hours of Medical Board investigator time researching this case, the accusation against me stated that the patient was homeless. Prosecuting attorney Bell had that amended at the opening of the hearing and documented the patient's address.

The patient's daughter gave the contact information to the personnel at Pomona Valley Hospital. When asked in the Medical Board Hearing why she didn't give her father's correct address, she testified that his former address at his ex-wife's home was in the hospital computer and the clerk neglected to change it. (Appendix #347)

At my request for a subsequent deposition, Pomona Valley Hospital Emergency Room Physician Gregory Burke, MD searched the hospital's medical records and found no previous record for patient BR. His name and contact information were not in the hospital database on February 6, 1998 when he arrived with his daughter.

The daughter gave the clerk the incorrect address, probably in an attempt to avoid the bill. Patient BR's multiple statements about his homelessness apparently were also designed to elude paying for medical services. The daughter lied about the existence of a previous chart on her father at Pomona Valley Hospital. This helped her explain the absence of his true address in the chart.

Many times during the hearing, Mr. Bell faulted me for neglecting to find out from the patient or his daughter that he had a home and a job. I have no way of knowing if he knew his witness was lying.

Medical Resident Dr. Ruth Karunananthan

When admitting patient BR, the Medical Resident, Dr. Ruth Karunananthan, used the abbreviation "PK" to stand for six-pack of beer. Mr. Bell argued that PK meant to indicate cigarettes. Dr. Karunananthan insisted that she referred to beer.

Despite all Mr. Bell's haranguing Dr. Karunananthan about her documentation in the chart of the patient's alcoholism, she stood by what she wrote in the chart and what she remembered—that the patient was an alcoholic.

102

Relevant Testimony of Ruth Karunananthan, MD, admitting medical resident, in the Medical Board Hearing (Appendix #347 Transcript, Vol. 1, Pages 191–7)

> Q. MR. ROSENZWEIG: Looking back on page 11, if you don't mind turning back to that for a moment. Going back to the alcohol reference, assuming that this information is true, that he was drinking one six-pack a day for 20 years—
>
> A. That's what he told me.
>
> Q. MR. ROSENZWEIG: Have you had experience in dealing with patients who had alcohol problems?
>
> A. Yes.
>
> Q. What's your definition of alcoholism?
>
> A. Drinking excessively.
>
> Q. Would this be, in your opinion, excessive drinking?
>
> A. For 20 years, six-packs?
>
> Q. Do you think that would be excessive?
>
> A. Yes.
>
> MR. BELL: Is this a moral judgment or medical judgment?
>
> MR. ROSENZWEIG: I'm not asking for moral judgment.
>
> THE COURT: Is this your medical judgment, what you're about to give? Is this your medical judgment?
>
> THE WITNESS: 20 years, a six-pack a day, yes. And, also, he had an abnormal liver function test when he came.

No reasonable physician would dispute that documentation of a six-pack per day of beer for 20 years in the medical history warrants a diagnosis of alcoholism.

Albert Yellin, MD, Anticoagulation Expert for the Prosecution

In the Civil Service Hearing, Dr. Yellin testified that I should have discharged the patient to a nursing home where he would be under the 24-hour supervision of nursing staff. He did not mention that, in an institutional setting under the constant care of medical professionals, it would not have been contraindicated to use warfarin (Coumadin) in an alcoholic. However, this testimony at the Civil Service Hearing was obviously used to counter my anticipated subsequent argument that alcoholism is a contraindication to the use of warfarin.

Unfortunately, at the time of the Civil Service Hearing, I did not know that the PDR designated alcoholism a contraindication to using warfarin. In any case, the patient had no condition that would have made him eligible for nursing home care, and he would not have agreed to nursing home placement. No nursing home would have wanted a patient being treated for active tuberculosis. No legal authority could have forced him to go to a nursing home.

At the Medical Board Hearing over a year later, knowing that I had discovered that alcoholism is a contraindication to warfarin, Dr. Yellin testified that, since cirrhosis of the liver was not diagnosed on autopsy, the patient was not alcoholic. He did not address Dr. Karunananthan's documentation of alcoholism when he testified that there was no contraindication to warfarin. He did not repeat his Civil Service Hearing assertion that I should have discharged the patient to a nursing home.

Testimony of Albert Yellin, MD regarding alcoholism (Appendix #348 pages 193–5)

> Q. MR. BELL: Is there anything in particular that you
> found in the chart that indicated the reasons for discontinuation of the anticoagulants, on the chart that had been written down?
> A. Nothing that indicated a valid reason for discontinuing it. Nothing that would be consistent with mandatory contraindications to anticoagulation. There are references to alcoholic

liver disease, things of that nature. There was no evidence this patient had any staged alcoholic liver disease.

There were references to alcoholism. I didn't see that corroborated any place in the medical record.

Q. He's been labeled to be an alcoholic. Is there— does this appear to be true based on review of the records?

A. I didn't see anything that would confirm it. The physical exam does not identify any of the stigmas of severe alcoholic liver disease, which is what we would be concerned about. A very mild abnormality of his liver function tests are readily explainable based on the medication he was taking, on the basis of his systemic tuberculosis. There is a note by an intern, I think about six something—about a pack times—

Q. One pack a day times 20 years, quit six months ago?

A. I think that which is stuck in the box for social habits, drinking. That is normally the way we refer to smoking habits, and I don't know whether that was a transposition. That's normally not the way we refer to people who drink. That's the only reference that I saw that would suggest alcoholism. But no other objective evidence that he was an alcoholic.

Q. What is alcoholic liver disease, or ALD?

A. The wastebasket term. It can be minimal amount of fatty infiltration of the liver or to the end-stage liver disease where you have a scarred, shrunken, shriveled liver with what's called "portal hypertension." This is an area of some research interest of mine. I've written a number of papers on it.

Q. You saw his liver was examined at autopsy?

A. Yes.

Q. It was not found to be consistent with cirrhosis?

A. That's correct.

Q. Was it found consistent with ALD?

A. I don't believe so.

There is no school of thought in medicine that maintains that alcoholism can only be diagnosed by a pathological finding of cirrhosis of the liver. Dr. Yellin knew what Dr. Karunananthan had documented in the chart, yet he gave false testimony in court that the patient was not alcoholic.

Excerpts of Decision by Administrative Law Judge H. Stuart Waxman (Appendix #351)

Factual Findings

The Pomona Valley records contained a number of inaccuracies. For example, they indicated BR had a history of homelessness 10 years prior and had been actually on the street for approximately eight weeks. In addition, BR's address printed on the records by the Pomona Valley computer was that of BR's former wife rather than his own address.

At 8:00 PM, BR was seen by Dr. Karunananthan who took a history. Dr. Karunananthan recorded a 50-pound weight loss in two months but failed to record BR's weight. She also recorded that BR had consumed one six-pack per day for 20 years, that he had quit drinking six months before, and that he was presently unemployed. All of those statements were untrue. Dr. Karunananthan also recorded that BR lived in a hotel but later crossed the statement out and wrote: "has home."

Where Dr. Karunananthan obtained the information in her history is in dispute. She testified she received all of the information in the history directly from her interview with BR's daughter, a substance abuse counselor who maintained a close relationship with her father, and testified to the inaccuracy of the

106

statements. She claimed, for example, that he drank considerably less than a six-pack per day and that he had not quit drinking prior to his hospitalization. **The discrepancy is relevant in that it was references to BR's substantial alcohol consumption, together with his elevated readings on liver function tests, which led Respondent to his erroneous belief that BR was an alcoholic.**

Neither Respondent nor any member of his team had discussed the matter with BR or his daughter, explained the risks and benefits of anticoagulation therapy, obtained information concerning the accuracy or inaccuracy of Respondent's perceptions of the risk factors BR presented, or obtained BR's consent for discontinuation of the anticoagulation medications. Had they done so, they would have learned BR had resided in his own apartment for many years, had worked as a cook in the same Kentucky Fried Chicken restaurant for many years, and **drank less than two quarts of malt liquor per day on weekends. (The evidence did not disclose his drinking customs during his workweek.)**

In this case, Dr. Yellin found nothing in the chart to indicate a valid reason for discontinuing the anticoagulation medications. . . .

Dr. Yellin also testified that it is improper to assume every homeless person will be non-compliant. A patient's homelessness only raises the level of concern but should not serve as a reason to discontinue anticoagulants. (According to Dr. Yellin, Respondent testified at the Civil Service hearing that BR was homeless, anemic, alcoholic, and suffered from liver disease and that these factors were contraindications for anticoagulation.) There was no evidence in the chart that BR was an alcoholic. A liver in a patient who was a heavy drinker for 20 years should show some signs of cirrhosis. BR's liver was examined in autopsy and found to be in a condition inconsistent with cirrhosis. . . .

Of the two experts who testified, Dr. Yellin was both more credible and more persuasive.

Legal Conclusions

Respondent was BR's physician and, as such, was obligated to be fully cognizant of each of the various factors which might affect a decision he made concerning his patient's care. Respondent failed to fully familiarize himself with his patient and the chart, relying instead on his team of interns and residents to orally advise him of factors essential to BR's care and treatment. Claiming he was too busy to read the chart (even though it was quite thin on February 9, when Respondent first became aware of the patient), Respondent read only a few portions and did not even look at the duplex scan from Pomona Valley.

In addition, Respondent based a life and death decision on erroneous information he could easily have verified by simply speaking with his patient. During his few visits with BR, Respondent was aware BR was able to converse and answer questions appropriately. Had Respondent informed him of his decision and the factors that contributed to it (i.e., concern about non-compliance, alcoholism, homelessness, lack of funds, etc.), BR could have provided accurate information and exposed the inaccuracies in the chart, thus enabling Respondent to make a fully informed and intelligent decision concerning the proper treatment of BR's DVT. Even Respondent's own expert testified that, if possible, the patient should be consulted in a case where an important decision such as the one in this case is to be made. If Respondent was convinced that BR could not intelligently participate in such a conversation, he need only have spoken briefly to BR's daughter, a substance abuse counselor, to learn the truth concerning BR's lifestyle. BR's daughter maintained a close relationship with her father and attempted to stay very involved in his care at the hospital. . . .

The purpose of an administrative proceeding such as this one is to protect the public from errant practitioners, and not to punish the licensee. (Camacho v. Youde (1979) 79 Cal.App.3d 161, 164) Respondent has been licensed to practice medicine in the State of California since 1977, and has no prior record of discipline. Ordinarily under such circumstances, in a case involving only a single patient, outright revocation would not be warranted.

However, that is not the case here. An additional factor exists in this case, which places the public at a far greater risk than would normally be expected in a case such as this. At the time of BR's death in February of 1998, Respondent was convinced that, despite a poor result, he had made the proper decision. Since that time, he has extensively researched the issue and has concluded that, because of the lack of evidence of effectiveness of anticoagulation in the treatment of popliteal DVT, he was absolutely correct in discontinuing the anticoagulants, particularly in light of what he perceived to be major risk factors (albeit not absolute contraindications). That reading of the literature appears to be completely at odds with the mainstream thinking of practicing physicians and researchers in the community. It is unacceptable for a physician to completely disregard the standard of care in the community simply because he (and very few, if any, others) believes the literature does not support it, to then discontinue the very treatment called for by the standard of care, and to fail to offer any effective alternative treatment.

Nonetheless, Respondent is now even more convinced than he was in 1998 that he made the correct decision in discontinuing the anticoagulant medication he had been approving for BR, and he made it very clear at the administrative hearing that, if faced with the same situation today, he would make the exact same decision. Respondent is entitled to that opinion. However, he is not entitled to foist that opinion on an unsuspecting public, more than 2,000,000 of whom suffer DVT annually. Those popliteal DVT patients who may be treated by Respondent in the future are now at even greater risk of pulmonary embolism than before because of Respondent's ongoing belief that the standard treatment for the condition, accepted by the vast majority of the medical profession, is nothing more than "dogma." No probationary order can adequately address and prevent that risk to the public. That risk to the public is too great to permit Respondent's continued practice of medicine.

ORDER

WHEREFORE, THE FOLLOWING ORDER is hereby made:

1. Certificate No. G-35122 issued to Respondent David Keith Cundiff is revoked.
2. Within ninety (90) days of the effective date of this Decision, Respondent shall reimburse the Board the sum of $39,338.69 for its costs of investigation and prosecution.

DATED: June 7, 2000

Appeal to the Superior Court of Judge Dzintra Janavs

My attorney Larry Rosenzweig prepared my appeal of the California Medical Board Decision. (Appendix #337) At my request, he focused on the alcoholism issue. (Appendix #338) For instance, the initial brief mentioned the following:

> Ms. Poole, BR's daughter, who has a malpractice suit pending against Cundiff, testified that her father was only a social drinker. (Tr. Vol. I, P. 440. On rebuttal, she testified her father drank almost two quarts of Colt 45 malt liquor per day on the weekends. (Tr. Vol. IV, Pp. 106-108,119).

However, he still wouldn't mention the size and alcohol content of a magnum of Colt 45 Malt Liquor because it wasn't entered into evidence. This really upset me.

In the memorandum replying to the brief of the prosecution, Mr. Rosenzweig again tried to drive the alcoholism point home:

> Dr. Yellin's statement that there is no evidence in the chart that Mr. BR was an alcoholic is not true. (Tr. Vol. II, P. 97, 166-167). Dr. Karunananthan's admission history and physical note checks "yes" in the box for alcoholism. (Ex. 4, P. 11). The absence of cirrhosis of the liver at autopsy in no way disproves the alcoholism of the patient.

Mr. Rosenzweig summarized my rationale for discontinuing the anticoagulants in the Supplemental Memorandum of Point and Authorities: (Appendix #339)

> Dr. Cundiff testified that he always gives anticoagulants to patients with a proximal DVT. (Tr. Vol. III, P. 179-180). However, a physician has to make a clinical decision based upon the whole patient, including medical, social, and institutional factors. (Tr. Vol. III. P. 174). In Dr. Cundiff's judgment, the risk of BR bleeding was higher than the risk of dying from a pulmonary embolism. (Tr. Vol. III, P. 139; Vol. IV, P. 33). The medical risk factors were an impaired liver function with increased baseline INR (an index of clotting factors made in the liver), (Tr. Vol. III, P.

140), anemia, and overall malnutrition. An elevated baseline INR indicates that the patient is more prone to bleeding with anticoagulants like Coumadin and heparin, which both affect coagulation proteins from the liver. (Tr. Vol. I, Pp.91-95). Consequently, the hospital anticoagulation protocol indicates that a patient with an increased baseline INR has to be watched very closely. (TR. Vol. II, Pp. 51-54). The house staff presented the social history as homeless, unemployed, uninsured, and alcoholic.

Dr. Cundiff was concerned about follow up with respect to monitoring the anticoagulation. Until the summer of 1997, the anticoagulation service was run by Dr. McGehee with two nurses. Patients came to Dr. McGehee's clinic for tests. The nurses called patients who did not show up for appointments. (Tr. Vol. III, Pp. 142-143). The pharmacy team which replaced Dr. McGehee's service only works on an inpatient basis. (Tr. Vol. III, P. 144). Outpatients have to come to one of three health clinics. At those clinics, a third of the patients do not show up and there is no system to make sure the patients come back. (Tr. Vol. III, Pp. 143-144, 195).

Judge Janavs' decision did not address my argument that alcoholism is an absolute contraindication to using anticoagulants and that the patient was documented to be an alcoholic. On the day of the hearing after the tentative decision was written, Mr. Rosenzweig held up a 40-ounce magnum of Colt 45 Malt Liquor to show Judge Janavs how much the patient drank.

She was not swayed. (Appendices #340a, #340b, and 340c)

I lost again.

Ms. Poole's Deposition in Her Civil Wrongful Death Case against Me

After the Medical Board revoked my medical license, the patient's daughter, Benita Poole, sued me for the wrongful death of her father. In a deposition related to this suit, the daughter testified repeatedly that she didn't know how much alcohol her father drank. When asked if she had ever seen him drunk, she said, "I'm not sure."

Since Ms. Poole filed a civil suit against me and the LA County Department of Health Services, the DHS had to provide me with legal representation to defend myself. I could no longer afford to pay for my own attorney. The case hung on the patient's alcoholism and Ms. Poole convinced Judge Waxman that, despite drinking up to two quarts per day of Colt 45 Malt Liquor per day on weekends, he was not an alcoholic. She convinced him also that my resident's history about homelessness and unemployment was faulty.

Relevant Testimony in Benita Poole's Deposition Regarding Patient BR's Alcohol Consumption (Appendix #358, Deposition Pages 20–21)

At my request, Mr. Richard Reinjohn (my County-appointed attorney) asked Ms. Poole questions in a sworn deposition on September 20, 2000:

Q. From your best recollection, from 14 to 19 years old, was your dad drinking?
A. At that age?
Q. Yes.
A. Yes.
Q. Was it a problem in the marriage?
A. No. No.
Q. When I say was his drinking—I understand how you're a substance abuse counselor.
A. Yes.
Q. We'll be more specific. What kind of drinking was he doing, to your recollection, when you were a teenager?
A. Social.
Q. What did that mean?
A. Whenever he had company or whenever he was watching a game.
Q. What was his alcohol of choice—
A. Well, I don't remember.
Q. During that time?
A. I don't remember.

Q. My kids also remind me of going to a bar function and hearing people say two scotches, please, and I don't drink scotch. Was your dad—did your dad drink hard liquor?

A. I really can't remember. I know he had before, but I can't remember if that was—

Q. During that time?

A. Yes. I can't remember.

Q. Were there any times as a teenager, do you recall, that your dad got drunk?

A. I'm not sure.

Q. Were there any times that you can recall when your dad had a problem, he acted up because of alcohol in his system?

A. No.

Q. Let me ask you a little bit about his—and this is the— let's say the year prior to his demise—what was his drinking habits like?

A. I only seen him drink on the weekends.

Q. What would he drink?

A. Beer.

Q. What kind of beer?

A. I don't remember.

Q. In your answers to interrogatories, you mentioned Colt 45.

A. Okay.

Q. Does that refresh your recollection?

A. It's possible.

Q. I didn't make it up. I got it from somewhere. Do you recall now that he drank Colt 45?

A. Yeah.

Q. Do you know approximately how much he drank on the weekend?

A. No, I don't. No, I don't. I'm uncomfortable with guessing. I can't tell you exactly how much he drank on the weekend.

Q. Did he drink single beers? You know, a 12-ounce beer? An 8-ounce beer?

A. I seen those before in his hand.

Q. What have you seen?

A The cans. The cans you're talking about?

Q. Okay. No. You tell me. I'm just giving some suggestions. You saw cans?

A. I don't know how many ounces the cans were, but I seen him drink a can of beer before.

Q So from the amount of time you seen him, he just drank one can of beer?

A. No.

Q. How much?

A. I can—can't say how much. Do you want to know how many cans?

Q. If you have any recollection of time or place, you know, specific, give it to me if you can. If you can estimate without guessing. I don't want you to guess or speculate.

A. I don't want to guess or speculate, either. I can't answer it without guessing.

Q. Did you ever see your dad drink more than one beer at any given time?

A. More than one can?

Q. A beer, period.

A. Yes.

Q. Did you ever see him drink anything bigger than a 12-ounce can?

A. Yes.

Q. What kind was that? How would you describe it? You know, nowadays, we have all these different shapes and sizes, so I can't guess. You got to tell me.

A. I don't want to guess. I don't know.

Q. Have you ever seen him with a glass container, like a Colt 45 glass container, that's bigger than your normal Coke bottle?

A. No.

Q. You know what a quart size is?

A. Go ahead.

Q. Now, you're a substance abuse counselor; right?

A. Correct.

Q. You're not like a normal—you know a little bit more than most people?

A. Okay.

Q. So we talk, you know, that there's definite sizes of alcohol cans; right?

A. Yes.

Q. Somebody tells you they had one drink, what comes to your mind?

A. I ask them to describe me what one drink is.

Q. Exactly. And when I say it to you, what do you think? What are you talking about when you say someone had one drink?

A. One drink is whatever you could consider one drink. Whenever you ask me one drink regarding my father, I'm thinking you're saying a can, if you mean one can.

Q. That's what you're thinking?

A. Right.

Q. Is that a 12-ounce can?

A. Yeah. Yes.

Q. On weekends, your dad would have more than one 12-ounce can?

A. Correct.

Q. During a 24-hour period, your dad would have more than one 12-ounce can?

A. Correct.

Q. And oftentimes, your dad bought not just the 12-ounce cans, but he bought the cheaper quart size, didn't he?

A. That's the bottle, yes.

Q You get more volume, cost less; right?

A. Right.

Q. Because, basically, you're paying for the container, not the stuff inside of it. And as we find out about water. That's why. What's the most you have ever seen him consume in a 24-hour period?

A. I seen him drink two of those bottles that I believe are quarts.

Q. Do you know what the alcohol content of a Colt 45 is?

A. Percentage?

116

Q. No. Do you know—do you know if there is any difference between the two?

A. Not really. I don't know.

Q. No drinking this now. This is a Colt 45 bottle. Do you know what size this is?

A. (She examines the bottle) It says 40 ounce, but if you would have turned it around and asked me to   guess, I would say a quart.

Q. Right. Your dad used to drink a bottle that looked like this; isn't that right?

A. Mm-hmm.

Q. That's a "yes"?

A. Yes.

The Medical Board case and my medical license hung on whether the patient was an alcoholic. On the issue of alcoholism, the daughter's subsequent sworn testimony directly contradicts her Medical Board Hearing testimony that directly affected the Judge's decision.

LA County District Attorney's Office Refused to Prosecute

I contacted the LA County District Attorney's Office to ask them to investigate my allegation that Ms. Poole had committed perjury. They replied that I had to take the matter up with the judge that heard my case. Consequently, I wrote to Judge Waxman, documented my allegation of perjury, and asked him to investigate. (Appendix #332)

> . . .My allegations of perjury against Ms. Poole relate to two issues that were essential to the case of the prosecution. The first issue is whether the patient was alcoholic. The prosecution conceded that Coumadin, the drug that I stopped, is absolutely contraindicated in alcoholics. Based on Ms. Poole's testimony, you ruled that Mr. BR was not alcoholic, and that I was negligent for failing to find that out. In a deposition leading to the financial settlement with the County of LA, Ms. Poole repeatedly testified that she didn't

117

know how much her father drank. When asked if she
had ever seen him drunk, she said that she didn't
know. Both these statements directly contradict her
sworn testimony in your courtroom—testimony on
which you based your decision. . . .

Administrative Law Judge Deborah Myers-Young answered for
Judge Waxman. (Appendix #359)

. . .There is no authority in the Administrative
Procedures Act for any Administrative Law Judge at
the Office of Administrative Hearings to work with
you in referring this matter to the District Attorney's
Office. Therefore, we will not be able to assist you.
You may contact the District Attorney's Office
yourself, or you may approach the Medical Board of
California to advise them of the situation.

Referencing this letter from the representative of Judge
Waxman, I sent my perjury documentation to the DA's Office.
(Appendices #334, and #335) Lieutenant Robert H. Hausken
answered for District Attorney Steve Cooley. (Appendix #360)

. . .Unfortunately, the District Attorney's Office
cannot respond to your request for a perjury
investigation at this time.

If Judge Waxman, having heard the testimony, was
not convinced that Ms. Poole was lying, it would be
extremely difficult for the prosecution to reasonably
expect to convince a criminal jury beyond a
reasonable doubt that Ms. Poole perjured herself.
Issues of her testimony should have been raised during
the hearing. . . .

He suggested that I hire a private attorney if I wanted to pursue
the matter. I could not afford to do that. I responded regarding
"Issues of her testimony should have been raised during the hearing,"
to Lieutenant Hausken. (Appendix #336)

. . .In the Medical Board hearing in May 2000, Ms. Poole testified unequivocally that her father drank less than the six-pack a day of beer that is documented in the medical record. She further testified that he drank up to two quarts of Colt 45 malt liquor per day on weekends. Judge Waxman referred to both of these statements in his decision, finding that BR was not an alcoholic and that I was negligent in failing to find this out.

The evidence of perjury came <u>four months after</u> the Medical Board Hearing before Judge Waxman. In a sworn deposition in her civil action that I sent you, she repeatedly said that she didn't know how much her father drank. Coumadin, the drug that I stopped, is absolutely contraindicated in alcoholics. . . .

I received no response from the LA County District Attorney's Office.

Chapter 11

Petitioning for Reinstatement
of Medical License

On March 9, 2009, I was finally ready to submit my petition to the Medical Board (Appendix #405) for the reinstatement of my medical license and to have the original revocation rescinded. The following is that petition. I began with a testimonial letter from Dorothy Jennings, sister of a Pain and Palliative Care Service patient to Richard Tannen, Chairman, Department of Internal Medicine. (Exhibit #1)

Date: October 16, 1992

Several months ago my brother was diagnosed with cancer of the lungs. During this period Dr. David K. Cundiff has followed him and has demonstrated much compassion and understanding with him and his special needs as a cancer patient. Dr. Cundiff's caring and dedication has made the crisis that has been brought to my brother and family a lot more bearable and though not easy, we are able to cope with the circumstances.

With the continued dedication he shows his patients and the special time he takes to talk with them and their families, I feel that the Department of Cancer Pain is vital for the patients and their families that need this service. It is services such as this that make me proud to say that I am an employee of the LA County + USC Medical Center where we do strive at "Being the Best" and more important, "We care."

I gave the Medical Board an excerpt of a book review of my book, *Euthanasia is Not the Answer—A Hospice Physician's View* (Humana Press 1992) based on my experiences on the Pain and Palliative Care Service. Jonathan Weisbuch, MD, then Medical Director of the LAC-DHS, wrote (Exhibit #3):

> Caring for patients whose diseases we cannot cure has declined in priority. David K. Cundiff is the exception. Trained as a cancer specialist, he has spent most of his career helping to manage pain, especially the pain of terminally ill cancer patients and those with AIDS. He has built a career on caring rather than curing. Caring is the subject of his book, *Euthanasia is Not the Answer—A Hospice Physician's View*, published by Humana Press. After assessing the physical, psychological, and emotional needs of patients who are going to die, Dr. Cundiff argues a caring plan which provides a pain free physical environment and supports the emotional, psychological, and spiritual needs of the patient will eliminate, if not completely prevent, the desire of the terminally ill patient to die prematurely either by suicide or with assistance by the physician.

I explained my duties as a palliative care medicine clinician and pain management researcher. I gave at least 200 continuing medical education lectures to medical students, nurses, physicians-in-training, and practicing physicians in California and other states. My service was one of the 10 highest volume such pain and palliative care services in the country. Since less than 20% of the 900 post-graduate physician trainees at the LA County + USC Medical Center had triplicate prescription forms, I required and the Drug Enforcement Administration authorized me to receive, 300 triplicate prescriptions per month. Because of the uniqueness of this Service in the safety net hospital with the largest volume of patients in California, I have written more prescriptions for opiate medication for cancer and AIDS patients than any physician in the history of the state.

Along with submitting about 15 more testimonials of patients, family members, and coworkers, I spent most of the rest of the

122

petition defending my decision to stop the warfarin in the patient in question. I would soon find out that this part did not go over well at all with Deputy Attorney General Klint McKay.

Conclusion of Petition for License Reinstatement

After submitting letters of support from six physicians, I concluded my petition with what Deputy Attorney General McKay called "defiance." (Appendix #405)

> The Medical Board case against me hung entirely on Ms. Benita Poole's testimony about her father's alcohol consumption and social history. Based on her deposition in the subsequent civil case against me and the deposition of Dr. Gregory Burke, it is clear that she committed perjury. Consequently, I seek not only to have my medical license reinstated but to have the original revocation rescinded.

Awaiting the Medical License Reinstatement Hearing

I submitted the petition for license reinstatement in March 2009. In April 2009, Deputy Attorney General Klint McKay sent me a letter (Appendix #379) saying, "You will not be permitted to attack the underlying revocation Order, the Proposed Decision, or any of the factual findings underlying it. . . ." Mr. McKay cited a legal precedent for a 30-day statute of limitations for appealing the ruling of the California Medical Board.

Since the depositions showing perjury of the star witness against me, the patient's daughter Benita Poole, were not completed for over a year after the Administrative Law Court Hearing, I thought that my new evidence should not be bound by that statute of limitations precedent. Having every intention of continuing to attack the facts and conclusion of the original case against me, I wrote to Attorney General Jerry Brown (Appendix #380) asking him to discuss my case with Deputy Attorney General McKay and provide guidance.

After the 90-day period for a check of my post revocation record, Deputy Attorney General McKay contacted me for a meeting to discuss my petition and my case. In July 2009, I met with Michael

Buttitta, the Senior Investigator for the California Medical Board, and Mr. McKay. I told Mr. McKay that I wrote to Attorney General Jerry Brown and, as requested, I brought Mr. McKay a copy of the letter. Mr. McKay knew but didn't tell me that Brown would not see my letter. Since my license reinstatement case was pending, the Attorney General's Office would send any correspondence concerning the case to the Deputy Attorney General on the case.

With my permission, they tape recorded the meeting and this was entered into evidence at the subsequent license reinstatement hearing.

Responding to questions by Mr. Buttitta and Mr. McKay, I reviewed the case used against me in the revocation of my medical license. I also told them about my teaching and practice duties at the LA County + USC Medical Center and my work on the Pain and Palliative Care Service. I highlighted my contention that the case against me was in retaliation for my outspoken criticism of the dysfunctional financing system of the LA County Department of Health Services that led to the closure of the Pain and Palliative Care Service and the resulting poor treatment of the terminally ill. After listening to all the background information, Mr. McKay asked me the big question: (Appendix #371, pages 39-41)

> MR. McKAY: So the basis upon which you terminated the warfarin was what? Tell me—tell me like distinctly exactly why.
> DR. CUNDIFF: Okay. That in my clinical judgment, this gentleman with alcoholism, liver failure, anemia, and in a social situation in which he, was—would have to go to clinics to get follow-up, for the monitoring of the Coumadin, and that that would be a major challenge for him. All of those factors, of course, with the risk of the Coumadin getting out of control, he was at greater risk in continuing the Coumadin than if the Coumadin was discontinued.
> MR. McKAY: And so you terminated it.
> DR. CUNDIFF: And so I terminated it.
> MR. McKAY: Now, as we sit here today, would you do the same thing?
> DR. CUNDIFF: Yes. And I told a judge that.

MR. McKAY: I'm trying to say, confronted with the same circumstances.

DR. CUNDIFF: Yes.

MR. McKAY: Okay.

DR. CUNDIFF: Confronted with the same circumstances, yes, I would do that.

MR. McKAY: Okay.

DR. CUNDIFF: And I think that, you know, according to my survey of other physicians would do the same. In fact, I found out after the civil service hearing and before the medical board hearing in my ongoing search of this medical issue, I read the package insert for Coumadin. And, package insert says that Coumadin is contraindicated in alcoholics and people with alcoholism.

And I said, "Whoa, that's a major thing." I mean, this judge in the civil service court didn't understand, that a physician has to make a clinical judgment about the whole picture.

But I think any judge can understand that if you have a patient that's documented to be an alcoholic and you have a drug that is dangerous and kills people and is contraindicated, that means you cannot do it.

If you do it, if anything bad happens—if he were to bleed in his head or have any other serious bleed from the Coumadin, that it would be malpractice for me to have continued that and send him home or to the downtown hotel. I would've had no wiggle room at all. I mean, as you know, if it's contraindicated and you do it and something bad happens, that's it.

MR. McKAY: So with respect to BR—

DR. CUNDIFF: Mm-hmm.

MR. McKAY: Do you—you don't think you made any mistakes in your treatment of him?

DR. CUNDIFF: No.

Mr. McKay's closing remark to me was, ". . .We're not going to discuss anything prior to the date of revocation, in all likelihood. That's typically what happens. We'll see. We'll see how it goes. . . ."

125

Reconsidering My Deposition Testimony to Deputy AG Klint McKay

After giving some more thought to my discussion about what I would do if faced with identical clinical circumstances as with patient BR in a future case, I emailed Mr. McKay and Mr. Buttitta (Appendix #372) with an elaboration on my answer. In that email, I said, "Instead of continuing the heparin and beginning the Coumadin and then stopping both after five days, I would have immediately stopped the heparin and not started the Coumadin." In my explanation, I cited two articles from the medical literature—my meta-analysis of venous thromboembolism trials showing clinical evidence of rebound hypercoagulation[1] and the Boston Brigham and Women's Hospital study[2] strongly suggesting rebound hypercoagulation in patients given prophylactic anticoagulation in hospital.

Soliciting Media Interest in the Case

About six weeks before the scheduled license reinstatement hearing, I called and emailed newspaper reporters and editors, trying to interest them in covering my case. The *LA Times*, *New York Times*, *Washington Post* and *Wall Street Journal* did not respond to my pitch. However, Joe Segura from the *Long Beach Press Telegram* interviewed me and filed a favorable article (http://www.presstelegram.com/news/ci_14922895). I asked my friends and supporters to write to Attorney General Jerry Brown including the *Long Beach Press Telegram* article to inform him about my case.

No one received a response from the Attorney General's Office.

Chapter 12

Medical License Reinstatement Hearing

On January 14, 2010, my hearing was held before Judge Daniel Juárez in an administrative law court in Los Angeles. Since I had no money to pay an attorney, I represented myself. My ex-wife, her husband, one of my daughters, and a housemate came to support me in the hearing.

The hearing began with the submission of documents to be considered as evidence. I started with the depositions of Ms. Benita Poole (Exhibit #10) and Dr. Gregory Burke (Appendix #361) that document perjury by Ms. Poole in the original hearing that resulted in the revocation of my license. Deputy Attorney General McKay objected to the admission of these depositions and produced a brief (Appendix #386) to back up his legal argument.

At my request, he had faxed me a copy of this brief the night before the hearing. Mr. McKay based his motion to bar the depositions on the legal precedent case establishing a 30-day statute of limitations imposed on appealing rulings of the California Board of Medical Quality assurance. To counter this argument, I said that the depositions were not taken until four months and 14 months after the hearing, so a 30-day statute of limitations would not be relevant. Mr. McKay's other legal argument was "Res Judicata," meaning that any decision from a court proceedings was final and facts and legal conclusions could never be subsequently challenged. In the brief, Mr. McKay wrote, "The truthfulness (or lack of) of Benita Poole does not support any exception to res judicata. . . .The rule is that fraud internal to the adversary proceeding, such as perjury committed during trial or error or mistake during the trial is intrinsic and not a basis for relief."

I told the judge that I searched the Internet for "res judicata, perjury exception, California" on Google.com and got over 11,000 hits. Judge Juárez ruled against me and did not allow the depositions into evidence.

The judge also disallowed my unsolicited letters of recommendation from patients and others concerning my work with the LAC+USC Pain and Palliative Care Service. (Exhibit #1, #20, #33, #39, and #40)

Mr. McKay objected on the basis that the reinstatement hearing had nothing to do with the quality of my medical care previous to the revocation of my license, but only to the evidence of my rehabilitation. Judge Juárez sustained the objection and barred the letters from evidence.

I then submitted for evidence a poll of internal medicine physicians and anticoagulation medicine specialists concerning the proper treatment of my patient. In this survey (published in my book *Money Driven Medicine—Tests and Treatments That Don't Work* (http://TheHealthEconomy.com/ChaptersMDM.pdf), Pages 407–418), physician opinions diverged markedly about the proper treatment and what would constitute malpractice. Mr. McKay objected that I was challenging the factual basis of the original malpractice conviction, and the judge sustained his objection.

I submitted my letter to Attorney General Jerry Brown (Appendix #380), asking Brown to be briefed on my case and for him to supervise Deputy Attorney General McKay. I made the case that I had a right to ask Mr. McKay to consult his boss on my case and for him to refuse was evidence of prosecutorial misconduct. Judge Juárez ruled that I had no right to request that Attorney General Brown, whose name was on every document sent by Deputy AG McKay, be consulted on my case.

I submitted an email from Mr. McKay to me (Appendix #381) responding to the letter that I sent to Attorney General Brown. He dodged my request that he consult his boss, AG Brown, and said, ". . . All of the issues which were litigated in the underlying case are irrelevant. . . ." Judge Juárez barred the email from evidence.

In submitting my published articles about the evidence-basis of anticoagulation as treatment of deep venous thrombosis, I made the case to Judge Juárez that my research and writing about this condition was my "rehabilitation." He accepted my articles.

Exhibit N: Anticoagulation Therapy for Venous Thromboembolism (http://www.medscape.com/viewarticle/487577) (*Medscape General Medicine*),

Exhibit O: Anticoagulants versus non-steroidal anti-inflammatories or placebo for treatment of venous thromboembolism (http://www.mrw.interscience.wiley.com/cochrane/clsysrev/articles/CD003746/frame.html) (*Cochrane Database of Systematic Reviews*),

Exhibit P: Clinical Evidence for Rebound Hypercoagulability After Discontinuing oral Anticoagulant for Venous Thromboembolism (http://www.medscape.com/viewarticle/582408) (*Medscape General Medicine*), and

Exhibit Q: "Systematic Review of Cochrane Anticoagulation Reviews" (http://www.medscape.com/viewarticle/582408) (*Medscape Journal of Medicine*).

Mr. Mc Kay objected to these articles being admitted, but Judge Juárez overruled him.

Next, I took the witness stand in my own behalf. Deputy AG McKay constantly objected if I brought up anything regarding a defense of my treatment of patient BR with the deep venous thrombosis. He and the judge both said they wanted to hear about my rehabilitation. I said that my research and published articles about venous thromboembolism was evidence of my rehabilitation. Over Mr. McKay's objections, I attempted to discuss the research articles that Judge Juárez allowed into evidence. Judge Juárez only let me read the conclusion sections of the abstracts.

Under cross examination, Mr. McKay directed the Judge's attention to the transcript of the interview that I had with Mr. Buttitta and Mr. McKay (Appendix #371, pages 45–46) the previous July:

> MR. McKAY: So with respect to BR—
> DR. CUNDIFF: Mm-hmm.
> MR. McKAY: Do you—you don't think you made any mistakes in your treatment of him?
> DR. CUNDIFF: No.

MR. McKAY: I'm trying to say, confronted with the same circumstances.
DR. CUNDIFF: Yes.
MR. McKAY: Okay.
DR. CUNDIFF: Confronted with the same circumstances, um, yes, I would do that.

Mr. McKay asked me again, in front of Judge Juárez, what I would do if confronted with the same clinical circumstances again as with my patient with deep venous thrombosis?

I said that my opinion had changed. I testified that instead of beginning the anticoagulants and then stopping them on day five, I would not start them in the first place. I pointed out to Mr. McKay that I had sent him and Senior Investigator Buttitta an email (Appendix #372) shortly after that interview, explaining in detail the basis of my changed opinion. Mr. McKay said he did not get the email and appeared shaken.

I proceeded to elaborate that my research on deep venous thrombosis treated with anticoagulants showed that, in the two months following discontinuing anticoagulants, there is a marked spike in recurrent episodes of leg and lung clots attributable to "rebound hypercoagulation." I said that my patient most likely died of rebound hypercoagulation caused by the anticoagulants rather than due to the lack of anticoagulant medication.

Mr. McKay appeared flat-footed. He had no expertise to dispute my testimony and had not arranged for an anticoagulation expert to testify. He also had no one to rebut my articles challenging the evidence-basis of anticoagulation for deep venous thrombosis that Judge Juárez allowed into evidence.

At the end of the hearing, I felt that it went very well. However, at the end of two of the three previous hearings, I also thought that I had won.

130

Decision by Judge Daniel Juárez: Deny License Reinstatement

Ruling that I was not "rehabilitated" due to my medical opinion about DVT treatment, Judge Juárez issued a "Proposed Decision" to deny the reinstatement of my medical license. (Appendix #377) He indicated that my unconventional thinking about the anticoagulation treatment of deep venous thrombosis made me a continuing danger to patients.

I submitted a petition for reconsideration of the Proposed Decision to the California Medical Board. (Appendix #378) However, without comment, the Board accepted Judge Juárez' Proposed Decision on April 22, 2010, denying my license reinstatement.

"Writ of Administrative Mandamus" to the LA County Superior Court

Using the official transcript of the hearing before Judge Juárez (Appendix #383) and the Decision, I next prepared my appeal to the LA County Superior Court by means of a "Writ of Administrative Mandamus." (Appendix #382) At this point, I gave up on fighting the "Res Judicata" legal doctrine that prevented a reconsideration of the original case. Instead, my appeal focused on my "rehabilitative" research and writing in the field of anticoagulation medicine, particularly my articles challenging the evidence basis for anticoagulation treatment of VTE.

Judge Juárez had admitted four of my peer-reviewed medical articles into evidence. I referred to those articles at the most crucial part of the hearing when Deputy Attorney General McKay asked me how I would treat a future patient with a DVT that presented exactly like my patient who died. I responded that, instead of beginning the anticoagulants on admission to the hospital and discontinuing them on day five, I would not begin the anticoagulants in the first place.

Justifying my changed opinion, I discussed my article on rebound hypercoagulability from Exhibit P, the *Medscape Journal of Medicine* article (http://www.medscape.com/viewarticle/582408), to argue that my previous patient most likely died due to the rebound clotting caused by my beginning and then stopping the heparin and warfarin.

I also discussed my other medical journal articles admitted into evidence (Petitioner's Exhibits "N," "O," and "Q") that challenged the evidence-basis of anticoagulation for VTE.

Deputy Attorney General McKay did not bring any medical expert witnesses to critique my published articles or to challenge the validity of my changed opinion about treatment of VTE. However, in the Decision, Judge Juárez wrote, "Saliently, if faced with the same clinical situation today, the Petitioner would essentially not act differently." (Appendix #377, LEGAL CONCLUSIONS #5)

Judge Juárez did not attempt to critique my claim that not beginning anticoagulants at all was significantly different from beginning and stopping the anticoagulants. This became the basis of my LA County Superior Court appeal. I also planned to find physicians to draft "declarations" to submit into evidence that supported my contention about the major difference between the two treatment options and my rehabilitative scholarship as evidenced by my medical journal publications in anticoagulation medicine.

Chapter 13

Researching Anticoagulation Clinical Science

Because of the malpractice allegation against me involving patient BR, I researched the evidence basis of anticoagulant treatment (blood thinners) for venous thromboembolism (VTE), including deep venous thrombosis (DVT) and pulmonary emboli (PE). The standard treatment for either DVT or PE is to give a fast-acting anticoagulant, such as heparin, in a vein followed by a daily vitamin K antagonist like warfarin (Coumadin) pills. This practice was established in the 1940s before the modern era of vetting experimental treatments with randomized controlled clinical trials.

After considerable searching, I discovered a randomized trial that was published in the medical literature in 1994. In this trial, two out of 48 patients that received standard anticoagulation (heparin and warfarin) died—one of PE and one of a heart attack. None of 42 DVT patients treated with an anti-inflammatory drug and no anticoagulation drugs died.[1,2]

I was shocked. In the hundreds of studies and review articles on DVT and PE that I had read, this trial had never been referenced.

Conflict of Interest in Anticoagulant Research

Wanting to know how blood thinners came to be considered the standard of medical care for DVT and PE patients, despite the lack of clinical science to support this treatment, I read the guidelines for the use of blood thinners in the American College of Chest Physicians (ACCP) Consensus Conferences on Anticoagulant Therapy. DuPont Pharmaceutical, makers of Coumadin, the top-selling brand of warfarin, underwrote the first six conferences (1985–2001).[3-8]

In 2002, DuPont sold its pharmaceutical business, including Coumadin, to Bristol-Myers Squibb. In 2001, before DuPont sold its pharmaceutical division, I sent Richard U. De Schutter, Chairman and CEO of DuPont Pharmaceuticals Company, an early draft of my review of anticoagulant therapy of DVT and PE, showing that

Coumadin was neither safe nor effective. The final draft was published in 2004.[9] Edward C. Bradley, MD, DuPont's Executive Vice President, ignored the substance of my letter in issuing DuPont's reply. (Appendix #407) I have often wondered if DuPont executives sold its pharmaceutical division because I alerted them to the tremendous legal liabilities of their drugs Coumadin and Innohep (a low-molecular-weight heparin).

Subsequently, the funding for the ACCP Consensus Conference on Anticoagulant Therapy in 2004 was described as follows:[10]

> The American College of Chest Physicians wishes to acknowledge the cooperation and support of the following sponsors for providing an unrestricted educational grant to support the publication of this supplement to *CHEST*: AstraZeneca LP; Aventis Pharmaceuticals; Bristol-Myers Squibb/ Sanofi-Syntholabo Partnership; GlaxoSmithKline; Organon Sanofi-Syntholabo LLC.

All these companies sell anticoagulant medications. Out of 92 authors of the anticoagulation guidelines, 63 acknowledged receiving money from these same companies for conducting research, participating on advisory boards, and/or speaking at educational events[11] besides their payments for drafting the guidelines. Similarly, the 2008 ACCP conference on anticoagulation uses was entirely underwritten by anticoagulant-producing drug companies.[12]

The Drug Regulators at the Food and Drug Administration

After failing to get an appropriate response to my challenge of the efficacy of anticoagulant treatment of venous thromboembolism from DuPont, I phoned Lilia Talarico, MD, Chief of the Food and Drug Administration (FDA) branch that investigates coagulation-related drugs. I asked her if she knew of any randomized trial of DVT patients that included a control group that did not receive anticoagulants that proved that anticoagulants reduce deaths. She told me that such a trial would be unethical because of the well-established evidence that anticoagulants were effective treatment for DVT patients. I then asked if she knew of the existence of the randomized trial by Nielsen and colleagues that showed no benefit with anticoagulants in DVT patients.[1, 2] She did not.

I sent the article concerning the Nielsen trial, my anticoagulant review article, and related materials to Dr. Talarico and her boss, Dr. Robert Temple, FDA Director of the Office of Medical Policy. They did not reply. However, through the FDA Ombudsman, Jim Morrison, they told me that they acknowledged the lack of randomized trial data supporting anticoagulants for treatment of DVT and PE. However, they believed that anticoagulants work in treating DVT and PE because, "rigorous, scientific trials show that they work in prevention of DVT."

Nonsense!

FDA approval requires scientific evidence of effectiveness for each individual indication for treatment. Randomized trials of elective surgery patients showing that low-dose anticoagulants prevent DVT as assessed by X-ray studies (a "surrogate" endpoint) do not constitute evidence that high-dose anticoagulant treatment reduces the chance of death or disability of those patients from DVT and/or PE (a "clinical" endpoint). Drs. Talarico and Temple extrapolated from this surrogate endpoint of preventing DVT in surgery patients to conclude that much higher doses of anticoagulants decrease the morbidity and mortality of patients who already have DVT and PE (a clinical endpoint for a completely different indication).

Anticoagulants for PREVENTION of VTE

Because Drs. Talarico and Temple at the FDA claimed that well-conducted scientific trials proved the efficacy of anticoagulants in prophylaxis (prevention) of DVT and PE in hospitalized patients, I studied that scientific evidence. Physician researchers have published hundreds of placebo-controlled trials. In patients undergoing major surgeries, using heparin and other anticoagulant drugs reduces the number of DVTs found on leg X-rays from about 50% of patients to about 10%–20% of patients (using a surrogate endpoint).

In an article entitled, "Prevention of Venous Thromboembolism," from the most recent ACCP Consensus Conference on blood thinners—Antithrombotic and Thrombolytic Therapy: *American College of Chest Physicians Evidence-Based Clinical Practice Guidelines (*8th Edition)—William H. Geerts, MD, and six

135

coauthors issued VTE prevention guidelines for various kinds of surgery patients.[13]

Since DVTs sometimes lead to PE, and PE sometimes leads to death, the drug company-financed researchers inferred that prophylactic anticoagulants prevent death. However, in reviewing the evidence-basis of these guidelines, I found that most of the DVTs discovered on X-rays in these research trials did not cause pain and resolved by themselves. None of these hundreds of trials included enough patients to show statistically significant evidence that prophylactic anticoagulants prevent death. Many published studies had no deaths from PE in either the anticoagulant treatment group or the placebo control group. Perhaps one in 2,000–5,000 hospitalized patients die of PE. Very few of the trials had more than 1,000 patients—not enough on which to base a clinical recommendation.

Dr. Geerts received research funding from anticoagulation drug producing companies Aventis Pharma and Pharmacia & Upjohn. His coauthors had also received financial support from those companies and, additionally, AstraZeneca, Corvas, DuPont Pharma, Wyeth-Ayerst Emesphere Technologies, Leo Pharma, and Rhone-Poulenc Rorer.

This represents a combination of faulty science and financial conflict of interest.

VTE Study at Boston's Brigham and Women's Medical Center

While trying to make sense of hundreds of randomized trials of anticoagulants used for prophylaxis, I discovered an article by Samuel Goldhaber, MD, and colleagues from The Brigham and Women's Medical Center, a Harvard-affiliated hospital.[14] In a chart review study, they tracked the incidence of developing DVT or PE after hospitalization in about 80,000 patients hospitalized over a two-year period. They expected to find more deaths in the patients not receiving anticoagulants for clot prevention while in hospital. To their surprise, 12 of the 13 deaths from PE occurred in the group that received anticoagulant prophylaxis. I performed a statistical analysis of their data and concluded that prophylactic anticoagulants actually increase the PE death rate by at least three times and as much as by 185 times.[15]

By email, I asked Dr. Goldhaber how many of the 20 patients that died of causes other than PE (e.g., advanced cancer and heart failure) had received anticoagulant prophylaxis. At issue was the likelihood that patients with underlying end staged diseases would be much more susceptible to dying of rebound hypercoagulation than healthy people. He sent me the number but, when I asked his permission to divulge the number in a letter to the editor about his study, he refused.

When I presented this information to the FDA in 2001, they still refused to conduct a serious investigation of the issue. Drs. Talarico and Temple would not even comment on the information that I presented to them.

Long-Term Anticoagulant Treatment for DVT and PE Patients

Paul Ridker, MD, an anticoagulation researcher from Harvard, convinced the National Institutes of Health (NIH) to spend $3.5 million to fund a placebo-controlled trial of long-term, low-dose warfarin (Coumadin) for patients who had previously sustained an episode of venous thromboembolism (either DVT or PE). After the standard three to six months of warfarin therapy, the drug would be continued at a lower dose indefinitely. *The New England Journal of Medicine* rushed to publish the study, "Long-Term, Low-Intensity Warfarin Therapy for the Prevention of Recurrent Venous Thromboembolism (PREVENT),"[16] because they claimed that this advance in treatment would have a significant positive impact on public health. Dr. Steve Rosenberg of the NIH, a coauthor of the trial, justified the expenditure of government money to expand the indications for warfarin because it is a generic drug, reasoning that drug companies could not afford expensive studies when the profit margin for drug sales is low.

After the *New England Journal of Medicine* refused to publish my commentary critiquing the PREVENT study, it appeared in *Medscape General Medicine* in July 2003.[17] I pointed out many scientific flaws with the study. None of the study authors or NIH monitors of the study would issue a public rebuttal to my criticisms. I wrote to Elias Zerhouni, MD, NIH Director, requesting a written reply to my commentary. He responded to my letter by saying that authors of publicly funded trials can choose whether or not to respond to published peer-reviewed scientific criticisms of their work. Without a rebuttal from the study authors, the medical media would not cover my commentary.

Cochrane Review of Anticoagulation Treatment for Venous Thromboembolism

In 2001, I volunteered to help conduct a review of anticoagulant treatment for venous thromboembolism for the *Cochrane Database of Systematic Reviews*. The Cochrane Collaboration is a project of volunteer medical researchers from all over the world that investigate randomized controlled trials and other scientific evidence in many areas of medicine to determine which treatments work and which do not. After thoroughly searching all the Cochrane databases and contacting anticoagulant experts and drug companies, their archivists turned up two other randomized, controlled trials of anticoagulation therapy in DVT patients.[18, 19] Neither trial found any benefit due to anticoagulants. Neither had been referenced in **any** articles or reviews of anticoagulant therapy that I read. The Cochrane peer-reviewers (four out of seven of whom had financial ties to drug companies that make anticoagulants) delayed four years before publishing this review.

Finally, in January 2006, Cochrane published the review entitled, "Anticoagulants or non-steroidal anti-inflammatories or placebo for treatment of venous thromboembolism"[20] by Dr. Juliet Manyemba, a physician from England, John Pezzullo, PhD, a biostatistician formally from Georgetown University School of Medicine, and me. The peer-reviewers and editor chopped out most of what we wrote in the discussion and conclusion of this review.

Our first draft of the "Implications for Practice" section stated, "Anticoagulants are not evidence-based to be safe and effective in reducing morbidity and mortality in patients with venous thromboembolism." For the "Implications for Research" section, we suggested conducting a non-inferiority randomized trial to compare standard anticoagulants with a nonsteroidal anti-inflammatory drug (NSAID) to see whether an NSAID (i.e., platelet inhibitor) could be equally effective but safer and less expensive. A non-inferiority trial tests whether a new or different treatment is statistically equal to or no worse than health outcomes compared with a standard treatment.

138

However, after editing by the peer reviewers and editor, the "authors' conclusions" were changed to: "The limited evidence from randomized controlled trials of anticoagulants versus NSAIDs or placebo is inconclusive regarding the efficacy and safety of anticoagulants in venous thromboembolism treatment. The use of anticoagulants is widely accepted in clinical practice, so further randomized controlled trials comparing anticoagulants to placebo could not ethically be carried out."

While the Cochrane peer-reviewers and editor delayed the publication of our evidence-based venous thromboembolism review, I sent a much more detailed and complete review to *Medscape General Medicine*. On September 9, 2004, *Medscape General Medicine* published my review challenging the safety and efficacy of anticoagulant treatment of venous thromboembolism[9] together with a podcast by chief editor Dr. George Lundberg entitled, "Is the Current Standard of Medical Practice for Treating Venous Thromboembolism Simply Wrong?"[21]

Again, no one from the academic or government anticoagulant establishment replied to the review or to my answers to the subsequent letters responding to the review and elaborating on my reasons for rejecting the additional evidence that Cochrane peer-reviewers initially wanted included.[9, 14, 22]

Anticoagulants for Patients with Atrial Fibrillation and Artificial Heart Valves

The 85-year-old mother of a good friend of mine took warfarin (Coumadin) every day. Her doctor prescribed the Coumadin because she had atrial fibrillation (i.e., an irregular heartbeat) and a porcine (pig) valve in her heart. One day she fell and hit her head. Over the next 24 hours, she deteriorated neurologically with lethargy progressing to coma. Medical evaluation revealed a large hemorrhage into her brain. Neurosurgeons evacuated the blood from this site by drilling burr holes through the skull. Over the next week she had little neurological recovery. She developed respiratory failure, which they treated with mechanical ventilation, and kidney failure prompting hemodialysis. Despite my efforts to advocate a palliative care approach, my friend's mother remained on life support until she died two months later. Her physicians determined that warfarin (Coumadin) anticoagulation led to the fatal bleed in her head.

My friend asked me what I thought of his mother's treatment, so I researched whether the FDA approval for this indication was based on any sound evidence. I found that the FDA guideline for warfarin for this medical indication is based on an extrapolation of randomized controlled trial evidence from patients with atrial fibrillation who did not have artificial heart valves.[23] Researchers have never published a clinical trial to see if warfarin is safe and effective for people with porcine heart valves and atrial fibrillation.

I filed a Freedom of Information Act (FOIA) request with the FDA on April 1, 2001 to get the medical evaluation documentation explaining why they approved warfarin for use in atrial fibrillation patients who have had a cardiac valve replaced. After following up on the request at least a dozen times, the response came June 1, 2006, with no apology for the delay. The FDA spokesperson told me what I already knew—there is no scientific evidence for this indication. The letter said, "The reviews done on the bioprosthetic valves seem to indicate a reliance on the recommendations of the American College of Chest Physicians. . . ."

The charge was $246.40. I didn't pay and they never came after me for the money.

Had my friend's mother not been given warfarin and then died of an embolic stroke (blood clot traveling from her heart to her brain), her doctor could have been sued for negligence based on warfarin's FDA approval for this indication. In people older than 80 years taking warfarin in one study, major bleeding occurred in 13% per year.[24]

This led me to wonder if the warfarin indication for atrial fibrillation patients *without* artificial valves was evidence-based.

Anticoagulants for Non-Valvular Atrial Fibrillation

The most common use of warfarin (Coumadin) is in patients with non-valvular atrial fibrillation. These patients do not have mitral valve disease or mechanical or porcine heart valves. These criteria exclude my friend's mother. About 3% of people over 65-years-old have non-valvular atrial fibrillation. About 3 million Americans have this indication for warfarin in 2011,[25] and at least 1.5 million non-valvular atrial fibrillation patients take warfarin each day.[26, 27]

140

Given the high bleeding risk of warfarin and other vitamin K antagonists, patients are remarkably poorly informed about it and unjustifiably trusting of their physicians. A study of atrial fibrillation patients from Europe showed that only 58% of men claimed to understand their treatment program and only 7% knew that vitamin K antagonist use is aimed at preventing strokes. This blood thinner treatment negatively impacted 67% of patients in terms of diet, socializing, career, and independence.[28]

The FDA approval for anticoagulant therapy in non-valvular atrial fibrillation patients was based on randomized trials conducted and interpreted by researchers hired by drug companies. My research published in *Medscape General Medicine* showed that major biases occurred in conducting the trials and in interpreting them.[29] For the following reasons, anticoagulants are not evidence-based to be beneficial to patients with atrial fibrillation:

- Randomized trial findings cannot be generalized to all atrial fibrillation patients, because less than 10% of the patients with atrial fibrillation from the participating institutions entered the trials.
- The patients included in the randomized trials were younger and they received superior anticoagulation monitoring compared with atrial fibrillation patients seen in general practice.
- Randomized trials significantly underestimate the bleeding risks of warfarin when contrasted with observational studies of general medical practices (i.e., atrial fibrillation patients receiving warfarin and not participating in trials).
- The five well-conducted randomized trials all had short follow-up periods (1.3–2.3 years) and high rates of permanently discontinuing warfarin (10% to 38% of patients). Adverse events were not monitored after warfarin was stopped, so researchers did not record "rebound hypercoagulation" related deaths and venous thromboembolism recurrences. (i.e., adverse events in the two months following drug discontinuation)
- The total number of atrial fibrillation patients in the five well-conducted randomized trials (n=3,298) was too low to be able to distinguish whether warfarin is better than aspirin.

141

- Warfarin clearly caused more major and fatal bleeding episodes than aspirin.
- From 1988 to 1999 the use of warfarin quadrupled on a per capita basis, but the incidence of embolic stroke (clot traveling from the heart to the brain) in greater Cincinnati from 1993–1999 remained the same (31.1 versus 30.4 per 100,000).[30]
- However, in the greater Cincinnati area, the incidence of anticoagulant-associated intracerebral hemorrhage (AAICH) quintupled during the 1990s in conjunction with increased warfarin use for the treatment of atrial fibrillation.[31]
- A recent observation study of 116,969 patients with United Health Care insurance coverage who were at least 40 years old and had a diagnosis of atrial fibrillation or atrial flutter showed no reduction in strokes in warfarin treated patients compared with those given aspirin or no blood thinner.[32]

My atrial fibrillation review concluded saying that given the risk and cost of warfarin and its unproven efficacy compared with aspirin, aspirin should be preferred over warfarin in people with non-valvular atrial fibrillation.[29] No one from the anticoagulation establishment replied to my review of anticoagulation prophylaxis for atrial fibrillation patients published in *Medscape General Medicine*. One group of previous reviewers of this topic, who had no financial ties with anticoagulant-producing drug companies, agreed with my conclusion.[33]

Yet the standard of care for atrial fibrillation remains to prescribe warfarin or risk a malpractice suit.

Warfarin for Transient Ischemic Attacks or Minor Strokes

In the same month that my patient died of clots to the lung, my inpatient medicine service at LA County + USC Medical Center received a 52-year-old man with a massive brain bleed due to warfarin. He had been transferred from the medical intensive care unit where he was in a "chronic vegetative state." The family agreed to a "do not resuscitate" status. He still received hemodialysis, but the family wanted to have this discontinued soon after he was transferred to my service. His 5-year-old daughter spent as much time as she could at her father's bedside, grieving. I felt especially sorry for the child's loss of her father. I cared for the patient for eight days. He died on the day after I left the service.

The patient had a history of a transient ischemic attack (TIA). His doctor had prescribed the warfarin to prevent more TIAs or a stroke. The FDA had not specifically authorized the use of warfarin for TIAs. Aspirin was generally recommended for stroke prophylaxis in this situation. However, the guidelines from the American College of Chest Physicians Consensus Conference allowed for warfarin prophylaxis in TIA patients in certain situations.[34]

In 2005, the *New England Journal of Medicine* published a randomized controlled trial comparing warfarin with aspirin in patients after TIAs or minor strokes. The trial was stopped early because 9.7% of patients on warfarin died versus 4.3% taking aspirin.[35] Still the authors of this drug company-funded study did not recommend that warfarin should be contraindicated in patients with previous strokes or TIAs. Two subsequently reported trials also showed no benefit with warfarin in people with previous strokes or TIAs.[36, 37]

How many other children have lost a parent or grandparent because of anticoagulants?

Anticoagulants for Coronary Artery Disease

The package insert for Coumadin (warfarin) states, "Coumadin is indicated to reduce the risk of death, recurrent myocardial infarction (heart attack), and thromboembolic events such as stroke or systemic embolization after myocardial infarction."

A meta-analysis of 31 randomized trials involving warfarin after myocardial infarction showed significant benefit compared with placebo but no significant benefit compared with aspirin,[38] a drug that is much less dangerous. These studies did not evaluate adverse events due to warfarin withdrawal in these patients in the two months after stopping the drug.[39] An evidence-based medicine approach should require that the FDA remove the indication for warfarin in myocardial infarction and coronary artery disease.

For patients with a recent heart attack, randomized, controlled trials show no benefit when heparin is added to aspirin.[40] Despite the absence of efficacy in randomized trials, the American Association of Chest Physicians still recommends intravenous or subcutaneous (under the skin) injections of heparin or low-molecular-weight heparin in higher risk patients immediately after heart attacks.[41]

Heparins for Atrial Septal Defects

The case of Ariel Sharon, Prime Minister of Israel, illustrates the risks of heparins. Mr. Sharon received enoxaparin (Lovenox), a low-molecular-weight heparin, after a small stroke that his doctors thought might have resulted from a 2 millimeter diameter hole in between the left and right atrial chambers of his heart. His doctors speculated that his first small stroke may have been due to a clot passing through the tiny hole in the heart and traveling to the brain.[42] Mr. Sharon also had a condition called "cerebral amyloid angiopathy," a disorder that weakens artery walls, increasing the risk of a stroke due to bleeding.[43] The cerebral bleed that resulted from his Lovenox anticoagulation (a low-molecular-weight heparin) has caused him to be in a vegetative state for over five years.

Anticoagulation with heparins of people with strokes associated with holes between the chambers of the heart has not been shown to reduce the risk of recurrent strokes or death.[44]

Fondaparinux (Arixtra): An Expensive Patented Anticoagulant

In 2001, the FDA approved fondaparinux, a direct thrombin inhibitor anticoagulant marketed by GlaxoSmithKline, designed to compete with heparins for prevention of DVT and PE in orthopedic[45-48] and abdominal surgical[49] patients. Unfortunately, the so-called "non-inferiority" randomized trials that won the FDA approvals included no placebo group and were only designed to show similar results as a low-molecular-weight heparin. Alarmingly, in each group of the abdominal surgery trial, one patient out of about 1,400 bled to death.[50] The FDA accepted these non-inferiority trials despite the major bleeding risk and the lack of evidence that heparin itself reduces mortality when used to prevent VTE (DVT or PE).

Martin H. Prins, MD, an epidemiologist from the Netherlands, participated on the steering committees and in obtaining funding from Santofi-Synthelabo and NV Organon drug companies for trials of fondaparinux (Arixtra) in treatment of DVT and PE.[50, 51] Based on the results of these two studies, the FDA approved fondaparinux for the treatment of DVT and PE on May 28, 2004. Anticipating this approval, Sanofi-Synthelabo announced the sale of Arixtra and Fraxiparine (a low-molecular-weight heparin) on April 13, 2004 to GlaxoSmithKline for about $360 million.[52]

Without disclosing his major financial stake in Arixtra and the importance to the Arixtra deal of continued acceptance of anticoagulants as evidence-based treatment for DVT and PE, Dr. Prins also served as a peer-reviewer for my Cochrane review of the evidence of effectiveness and safety of anticoagulants in the treatment of VTE. I discovered Dr. Prins' role in these studies when I read the Arixtra DVT and PE trial reports.

Dr. Prins recommended that Cochrane should not publish my venous thromboembolism review. In large part because of his opposition to this review, it took about four years for Cochrane to publish the review, and then the results, discussion, and conclusion were largely written by the peer-reviewers and editor rather than by me and the other authors. Publication of the review that we originally submitted in the prestigious Cochrane Library in 2004 could have stopped the FDA from granting Sanofi-Synthelabo the indications for fondaparinux (Arixtra) for patients with DVT and PE.

I reported to Gerry Fowkes, MD, coordinating editor of the Cochrane Peripheral Vascular Disease Group, that Dr. Prins had this conflict of interest. I expected that he would disclose Dr. Prins' conflict of interest with the publication.

Dr. Fowkes didn't disclose Dr. Prins' financial conflict but did report mine medical malpractice case as a conflict of interest.

"Evidence-based Medicine and the Cochrane Collaboration on Trial"

A few months after the Cochrane Collaboration published their highly edited version of the review of anticoagulation treatment of venous thromboembolism that I coauthored, Dr. Kay Dickersin, Director of the U.S. Cochrane Center, emailed me and other Cochrane authors asking us to defend evidence-based medicine against an attack by Dr. Bernadine Healy. Dr. Healy, former Director of the National Institutes of Health, wrote an essay entitled "Who Says What's Best?" This piece, critical of evidence-based medicine, appeared on September 11, 2006 in *US News and World Report*.[53]

Instead of defending evidence-based medicine, I wrote a commentary entitled, "Evidence-based Medicine and the Cochrane Collaboration on Trial," detailing the biases and financial conflicts that I faced in researching and writing the Cochrane venous thromboembolism review.

I sent Dr. Dickersin this commentary and told her my story. She advised me to submit a formal complaint to the Cochrane disputes editor about the matter, so I did. When my complaint was not addressed for six months, I submitted the commentary to *Medscape General Medicine*.[54] I concluded the essay with an appeal for readers to email FDA anticoagulation experts asking for an investigation of the indication for anticoagulants for venous thromboembolism. At least 20 people emailed FDA anticoagulation experts.

Dr. Ellis Unger, Deputy Director of the Office of Surveillance and Epidemiology, called me to discuss the issue. However, the FDA still refused to investigate. They seemed to be delaying their final decision to see if the medical media would pick up the story. None of the medical journalists that I emailed reported on the article and letter-writing campaign asking the FDA to investigate.

My Review of Cochrane Anticoagulation Reviews

These experiences with the Cochrane venous thromboembolism review and the FDA made me wonder about the validity of research in other areas of anticoagulation medicine. I decided to systematically critique all the Cochrane reviews and protocols involving anticoagulant drug interventions to see whether other methodological errors, biases, and undisclosed financial conflicts exist.

I found that 57 anticoagulation reviews and protocols besides mine had been published by the Cochrane Collaboration. I sent a critique to the authors of each review and protocol. Only 13 of the 57 authors replied to my letters. Several complained that they were too busy. Others just ignored me.

By analyzing each review or protocol including mine and the response of authors, if any, to my letters, I found 207 total instances of methodological errors (divided into nine categories) and 18 total instances of biases (grouped into four categories). There were also 13 editors and 37 authors with undisclosed financial conflicts.

I submitted my findings first to *JAMA*, then to the *New England Journal of Medicine*, and finally to the *BMJ (British Medical Journal)*. Only the *BMJ* sent it for outside peer review. The two reviewers, one with major ties to anticoagulant-producing drug companies, rejected it. The *Medscape Journal of Medicine* (same journal that published my other papers, now under a new name) published my article, *"Systematic Review of Cochrane Anticoagulation Reviews,"* in January 2009.[55] In all, the review challenged the evidence-basis of warfarin and other vitamin K antagonists, heparins, and direct thrombin inhibitors (e.g., fondaparinux) for 30 FDA-approved and off-label indications.

By email, I pointed out the review to about 40 Cochrane anticoagulation authors and about 120 other anticoagulation researchers. None rebutted anything in the review. Again the medical media would not cover the issue.

Undisclosed Financial Conflicts of Interest in Anticoagulation Guideline Authors

An article from a health care blog about a dispute between Cathleen DeAngelis, MD, the editor of *JAMA*, and a whistleblower who reported an undisclosed financial conflict of interest of a *JAMA* author, led me to write to three medical journals about financial conflicts of their anticoagulation medicine authors. In emails to Dr. DeAngelis, Jeffrey Drazen, MD, the chief editor of the *New England Journal of Medicine*, and Rita Redberg, MD, the chief editor of the *Archives of Internal Medicine*, I detailed evidence that 31 of their authors did not disclose their payments from drug companies for drafting anticoagulant guidelines for the American College of Chest Physicians published in the journal *Chest*.

Dr. DeAngelis refused to require acknowledgments from *JAMA* anticoagulation medicine authors because the disclosure of financial support for the guidelines in *Chest* did not specifically say that the authors received direct payments. Here is what the journal *Chest* reported:[12]

> The American College of Chest Physicians wishes to acknowledge the cooperation and support of the following sponsors for providing an unrestricted

educational grant to support the publication of this
supplement to *Chest*: AstraZeneca LP; Aventis
Pharmaceuticals; Bristol-Myers Squibb/Sanofi-
Syntholabo Partnership; GlaxoSmithKline; Organon
Sanofi-Synthelabo LLC (2008).

At the request of Dr. DeAngelis, I emailed Richard S. Irwin, MD,
FCCP, *Chest* Editor-in-Chief, and Jack Hirsh, MD, FCCP, Chair
American College of Chest Physicians Evidence-based Practice
Guidelines. I asked about the lack of disclosure of payments from drug
companies to *Chest* authors for drafting anticoagulant guidelines.
They did not reply to me. Although I copied Dr. DeAngelis in that
email, she did nothing.

When I sent Dr. Rita Redberg a similar email about financial
conflicts of *Archives of Internal Medicine* authors, she contacted Dr.
DeAngelis (both *JAMA* and the *Archives of Internal Medicine* are
American Medical Association journals) and used the same reason not
to require disclosure.

Dr. Drazen replied to my letter about undisclosed financial
conflicts of *New England Journal of Medicine* authors by saying: "If
an author has received payments for work on guidelines from an
official organization, such as an established professional society that
sponsored the guidelines, disclosure is not required."

After all three editors stonewalled, I contacted some health care
reporters about these financial conflicts. They declined to investigate.

**My Letter to Dr. Janet Woodcock, the Director of the FDA Center for
Drug Evaluation and Research**

Subsequently, I drafted an email to Janet Woodcock, MD, the
Director of the Center for Evaluation and Research of the FDA,
asking for her to investigate my challenges to the evidence-basis for 30
indications for anticoagulants. The letter began:

I am asking you to consider conducting a transparent
investigation of the evidence I presented in "A
Systematic Review of Cochrane Anticoagulation
Reviews" challenging the evidence-basis for
anticoagulant use for 30 FDA-approved and off-label

indications
(http://www.medscape.com/viewarticle/584084).[55] This
review was based on my letters to authors of 57
Cochrane anticoagulation reviews pointing out
methodological errors, biases, and undisclosed
financial conflicts and my own Cochrane review of
anticoagulants for venous thromboembolism.[20] Only
13 of those Cochrane authors replied to my letters
critiquing their reviews. At least 50,000 people
worldwide bleed to death yearly from anticoagulants
used for those 30 indications.

Copies of the email went to about 150 people including:

- Editors of medical journals that have published articles
  supporting the use of anticoagulants for the 30 indications
  that my review challenges. In many of those articles, the
  authors have undisclosed financial conflicts of interest;
- Authors and editors of Cochrane reviews of anticoagulation
  prophylaxis and treatment interventions;
- Authors of antithrombotic and thrombolytic therapy
  guidelines published in eight supplements of the journal
  Chest[56-59] under the auspices of the American College of Chest
  Physicians;
- Other antithrombotic and thrombolytic therapy researchers;
  and
- FDA and NIH experts in antithrombotic and thrombolytic
  therapy.

The only initial response to my letter to Dr. Woodcock came from
Dr. David Tovey, the new Chief Editor of the Cochrane Collaboration
as of January 2009. He said that Cochrane takes feedback such as
mine seriously and committed to spend a week to draft a response to
all my feedback letters and to circulate that response within Cochrane.
By mid-June 2009, he planned to send me the result.

As of 2011, he has not responded to the content of my critiques of
Cochrane anticoagulation reviews. Periodically, he emails me that he
is working on getting his authors to respond.

Cost of Anticoagulation in Lives and Money

Venous Thromboembolism (DVT and PE) Diagnostic Tests

Of patients suspected of having DVT and PE, about 42%[60] and 25%[61] respectively have them diagnosed on imaging tests. About 300,000 U.S. residents are diagnosed with venous thromboembolism per year,[62] with approximately 90% of clinically diagnosed cases being DVTs. Consequently, about 600,000 and 120,000 people undergo diagnostic tests for DVT and PE, respectively. When pulmonary angiography (X-ray dye test) was routinely used in questionable PE cases, about 1/200 patients died of complications of this procedure,[61] causing hundreds of deaths per year. Now chest CT scans are considered definitive by more experts and pulmonary angiography deaths are less common.

Articles in the medical literature estimated the cost in 1992 of hospital tests for diagnosing DVT at $2,250 and PE at $4,333.[60, 63] This translates to about **$2 billion** in 1992 for diagnostic tests for venous thromboembolism. Because competition and efficiencies may have controlled the costs of these tests, and more recent data are not available, I used the conservative assumption of no inflation in the bills for these procedures since 1992. The cost may be much higher.

Warfarin and Other Vitamin K Antagonists

Calculating from rates of major and fatal bleeding due to warfarin and other vitamin K antagonists from observational studies (major bleeding: 2.3 –7.2% and fatal bleeding: 0.8%– 1.2%,[64-69] for about 4 million Americans using these drugs in 2008,[27,70] 92,000–290,000 people had major bleeds and 32,000–48,000 bled to death.

Extrapolating population-based data from the greater Cincinnati area (population = 1.3 million) to the entire country, about 22,000 Americans will have warfarin-related brain hemorrhage in 2011. This estimate assumes that the increase in warfarin prescriptions from 1998 (21 million) to 2004 (31 million) [30] has continued to rise at the same rate (7.8% per year). About 14,500 of those people (66%) will be dead within one year.[71] Most of the rest will remain permanently disabled.

The estimated cost for treating a patient with warfarin or other vitamin K antagonists in 2011 is about $1,100.[72,73] For total U.S. costs of warfarin treatment, this translates to about $4.4 billion ($1,100 for warfarin and monitoring x 4 million people taking vitamin K antagonists[27,70] = $4.4 billion). Since the U.S. accounts for about half of the world market for vitamin K inhibitors,[74] the total estimated warfarin costs for 2011 is about $8.8 billion.

The estimated average cost of bleeding from warfarin for 2011 is $2.8 billion–$8.6 billion (4 million people taking vitamin K antagonists[70] x $30,000 per major bleed[73,75] x 0.023–0.072 (proportion with major bleeds/year)[76] = $2.8–$8.6 billion).

In total, Americans will spend **$9 billion–$15 billion** on vitamin K inhibitor prophylaxis and treatment in 2011.

A new generation of oral stroke prevention drugs are being approved by the FDA based on noninferiority randomized trials in comparison with warfarin. The FDA approved Pradaxa (dabigatran), manufactured by Boehringer Ingelheim Pharmaceuticals Inc. on October 19, 2010.[77] Apixaban by Bristol-Myers Squibb and rivaroxaban, owned by Bayer HealthCare and under development jointly with Johnson & Johnson, are on track for FDA approval soon. Investment bank analysts estimate that this new generation of stroke prevention drugs could generate $10 billion or more in annual global sales[76] compared to *only* $8.8 billion for warfarin and other vitamin K inhibitors.[27, 70, 74]

Treatment with Heparins and Direct Thrombin Inhibitors: Bleeding Deaths

Based on a systematic literature review, the average *daily* frequencies of fatal, major, and total bleeding during full-dose heparin therapy for venous thromboembolism were 0.05%, 0.8%, and 2.0%, respectively.[66] Petersen and colleagues reported the daily rate of major bleeding due to heparin or low-molecular-weight heparin for acute coronary syndromes as 0.66%.[78] Consequently, applying these rates for approximately 3 million full-dose heparin courses (average 7 days) in the United States, **138,000 to 168,000 people had major bleeding** (3 million people x 0.0066 to 0.008 (major bleed risk/day) x 7 days = 138,000–168,000) and about **10,500 died of hemorrhage** (3 million people x 0.0005 (fatal bleed risk/day) x 7 days = 10,500).

While major bleeding rates are generally reported in studies of acute coronary syndrome patients treated with antithrombotics, they rarely report bleeding deaths. In a few studies of acute coronary syndrome patients, deaths attributable to bleeding may be deducted by comparing the 30-day death rate of those patients with major bleeding to patients with no bleeding. Deaths due to bleeding from anticoagulants for patients with acute coronary syndrome can be estimated by multiplying the difference between the death rate in bleeders and non-bleeders by the rate of major bleeding (Table 1).

Table 1. Deaths Attributable to Bleeding in Patients with Acute Coronary Syndrome

Study author	N	Deaths bleed %/ no bleed %	Major bleeds %	Death rate attributable to bleeding %
Rao[79]	24,112	8.0/3.08	10.0	0.492
Moscucci[80]	23,112	18.6/5.1	3.0	0.405
Segev[81]	5,842	19.2/1.5	1.4	0.248
Eikelboom[82]	34,146	12.8/2.5	2.3	0.237

Applying these rates of deaths attributable to bleeding to approximately 3 million people treated with high-dose heparins for acute coronary syndrome, percutaneous coronary interventions, and venous thromboembolism gives about **7,000–15,000 deaths** attributable to heparins and direct thrombin inhibitors (3 million x 0.00237–0.00492 = 7,110–14,760). This range is consistent with the estimate based on the meta-analysis of anticoagulation trials for venous thromboembolism (i.e., 10,500).

Prophylaxis with Heparins and Direct Thrombin Inhibitors: Bleeding Deaths

Low-dose heparin, low-molecular-weight heparin, and fondaparinux are used for venous thromboembolism prophylaxis. A review of 52 randomized trials that studied venous thromboembolism anticoagulant prophylaxis (n = 33,813) showed that low-dose heparins approximately doubled the rates of hemorrhage (0.28% versus 0.14%), including major bleeding of the gastrointestinal tract (26/12,928 = 0.2%) and retroperitoneum (10/12,642 = 0.08%).[83] The researchers did not report fatal and intracranial bleeding. Based on these data, for the 6 million hospitalized people given low-dose heparin, low-molecular-weight heparin, fondaparinux, or other anticoagulants in 2008 for venous thromboembolism prophylaxis in the U.S.,[84,85] at least 8,400 developed anticoagulant-related major bleeding (6 million x 0.0028 x 0.5 = 8,400).

An unknown number bled to death. If 1/1,430 people given a low-dose, low-molecular-weight heparin or fondaparinux prophylaxis bleed to death, as occurred in both arms of a non-inferiority trial comparing these two drugs,[49] then about 4,200 Americans bleed to death per year from anticoagulant drug prophylaxis.

Heparins and Direct Thrombin Inhibitors: Rebound Hypercoagulability Related Deaths

While major bleeding is a significant risk with low-dose heparin and other anticoagulants in venous thromboembolism prophylaxis, rebound hypercoagulability is possibly an even greater risk. My recent article with coauthors Paul Agutter, MD, Colm Malone, MD, and John Pezzullo, PhD (detailed below) estimated that about 15,000 people in the U.S. (95% confidence interval: 5,000–40,000) and 30,000 worldwide (95% confidence interval: 10,000–80,000) die of rebound clotting per year due to anticoagulants for prophylaxis and treatment.[86]

Prophylaxis and Treatment with Heparins and Direct Thrombin Inhibitors: Financial Costs

The estimated cost of a five-day course of low-dose, low-molecular-weight heparin prophylaxis or direct thrombin inhibitors (drugs, nursing, and pharmacy costs per patient = $343[73,87]) for 6 million hospitalized medical and surgical patients in 2011 will be about $2 billion ($343 each x 6 million = $2.06 billion). The cost of administering these drugs used in high doses for about 3 million people with venous thromboembolism, acute coronary syndromes, and other indications was at least another $2 billion. Treatment of bleeding from heparins will cost Americans an additional $5–$6 billion.[66,73,78,88] Of that, about $1 billion will be for bleeding from low-dose prophylaxis[73,88] and $4 billion–$5 billion for high-dose treatment (138,000 to

168,000 people with major bleeding from high-dose heparins[66, 78] x $30,000 per major bleed[73,75] = $4.1 billion – $5.0 billion).

Overall, heparin, low-molecular-weight heparin, and direct thrombin inhibitor prophylaxis and treatment in 2011 will cost Americans $8–$9 billion. And total cost of anticoagulant prophylaxis and treatment in the U.S. will be $17 billion–$25 billion in 2011.

A Cochrane Consumer Volunteer from Australia Makes Contact

Out of the blue in early April 2010, an Australian Cochrane Collaboration consumer volunteer, Peter Darroch, emailed me concerning my commentary in 2007 about my dispute with Cochrane. (http://medgenmed.medscape.com/viewarticle/557263) After he learned more about Cochrane's role in biasing reviews about anticoagulants and the financial conflicts of interests of the Cochrane reviewers and editors, he wanted to see that the truth came out about the efficacy and safety of anticoagulants for VTE.

Since Mr. Darroch was simultaneously corresponding with Dr. Iain Chalmers, a cofounder of the Cochrane Collaboration, I also got to meet Dr. Chalmers via email. After reading my story, Dr. Chalmers, too, felt concerned that the Cochrane administration was ignoring my criticisms of its anticoagulation reviews. He emailed Dr. David Tovey, the current Chief Editor of the Cochrane Collaboration, asking him to publish the promised Cochrane report on my *"Systematic Review of Cochrane Anticoagulation Reviews."*[55] Within a week, the Cochrane website published Dr. Tovey's report.[89]

Unfortunately, Dr. Tovey dealt only with Cochrane's *process* of addressing my feedback letters. He didn't rebut or criticize my published review of Cochrane anticoagulation reviews. He said: "I do not intend here to comment in detail about the content of the feedback, which is more properly addressed by content experts." However, the Cochrane authors and editors (i.e., content experts) never did respond to the content of my feedback letters and criticisms of their anticoagulation reviews. Dr. Tovey promised to ask the anticoagulation authors and editors to respond to the content of my criticisms after the publication of his response about Cochrane's process of dealing with my criticisms. However, eight months after his request to his authors (August 2010), they have not responded.

"Diet as prophylaxis and treatment for venous thromboembolism?"

Dr. Colm Malone, a British surgeon and long-time researcher into the cause of deep venous thrombosis, found one of my articles on anticoagulation and contacted me by email in February 2010. Along with his friend and research collaborator Dr. Paul Agutter, Dr. Malone wrote a book entitled, *The Aetiology of Deep Venous Thrombosis: a Critical, Historical and Epistemological survey*[90] Dr. Malone quickly introduced me to Dr. Agutter, the Chief Editor of the BioMed Central journal *Theoretical Biology and Medicine Modeling*, and we began collaboration on a proposed journal article.

In their book, Drs. Malone and Agutter challenged medical orthodoxy about the cause of DVT and introduced their alternative theory of causation called, "venous cusp hypoxia hypothesis."

Since the 1960s, the medical community has accepted that DVTs are caused by the so-called "Virchow's Triad," a combination of

- damage to the vein's inner wall,
- blood stasis, and
- "hypercoagulability" (extra sticky blood).

The hypercoagulability component of Virchow's Triad served as the theoretical basis for the advent of the pharmaceutical industry launching an incredibly massive and lucrative initiative from the 1960s until now, with anticoagulant drugs as prophylaxis and treatment for VTE.

In opposition to this Virchow's Triad, the venous cusp hypoxia hypothesis maintained that hypercoagulability was not a part of the cause of DVT, leaving damage to vein walls at the sites of valve cusps and blood stasis as the dual causes. These valve cusps tend to be most susceptible to being in a low-oxygen environment and sustaining hypoxic injury, especially when upward blood movement is slow in the legs (blood stasis). Veins, particularly dependent veins in the legs, have valves to help massage the venous blood's uphill trek back to the heart. Valves in leg veins serve as partitions that keep blood from backing down due to the downward pressure of gravity.

Previous to our collaboration, Drs. Malone and Agutter had been suspicious of the value of anticoagulation for prophylaxis and treatment of DVTs, but had not openly challenged medical orthodoxy on this point. They are basis scientists interested in pathophysiology and causation of DVT. My articles disputing the evidence-basis for efficacy of anticoagulation for prophylaxis and treatment of VTE made them eager to work with me to further explore the use of anticoagulants for VTE. For help with the statistical aspects of the project, we enlisted the help of Dr. John Pezzullo who had previously been my coauthor in the Cochrane review of anticoagulation for VTE.[20]

Our article entitled, "Diet as Prophylaxis and Treatment for Venous Thromboembolism?" *was* published August 11, 2010 in the medical journal *Theoretical Biology and Medical Modelling*.[91] It updated the data in my previous articles and more strongly challenged the efficacy and safety of anticoagulants for prophylaxis and treatment of VTE.

This article spelled out in statistical detail how anticoagulant prophylaxis and treatment for venous thromboembolism (VTE) do not decrease clotting deaths. Instead, these drugs cause up to 40,000 bleeding and rebound clotting deaths per year worldwide, up to 20,000 of which occur in the U.S.

Indeed, rebound hypercoagulability is the most likely reason that my patient BR died about a week after I stopped his heparin and warfarin (Coumadin).

In addition to showing that anticoagulants caused harm when used for VTE prophylaxis or treatment, we reviewed the medical literature about the relationship of diet to VTE. We found that a more plant-based diet would decrease the risk of developing VTE versus a more animal-based diet. Finally, we proposed randomized controlled non-inferiority clinical trials to compare standard anticoagulant treatment with potentially low VTE risk diets (i.e., vegan, vegetarian, or Mediterranean diets).

After publication of the article, I emailed at least 100 academic anticoagulation experts and U.S. Department of Health and Human Services (i.e., Food and Drug Administration and National Cancer Institute) regulators, inviting them to comment on the article with their critiques. While over 1,300 people looked at the article on the BioMed Central website and more on the PubMed website, only one reader commented on it.[91] That comment did not rebut any of the points about the ineffectiveness of anticoagulants in preventing thrombosis deaths and the massive toll of bleeding and rebound clotting deaths caused by anticoagulant prophylaxis and treatment.

Conclusion

Historical precedent, observational studies, and methodologically flawed randomized controlled trials have constituted the evidence for anticoagulant efficacy. Anticoagulant therapy for a variety of diseases has been promoted to the medical profession and public by pharmaceutical company money spent on research, continuing medical education programs by drug company funded researchers, medical journal advertising, lobbying, and marketing.

Unless this doctor-caused (iatrogenic) epidemic is stopped by the FDA and NIH, at least 100,000 humans worldwide will die of anticoagulants in 2011. From 40,000–60,000 Americans will die in 2011 due to bleeding from anticoagulants. Tens of thousands more will die of rebound hypercoagulation after stopping anticoagulant drugs. Anticoagulant treatment and prevention of clots will cost between $17 billion and $25 billion in 2011 in the U.S. alone. The worldwide toll of major bleeds and deaths is about double that in the U.S.

If anticoagulant treatment were eliminated in America, it would end a very expensive and deadly iatrogenic epidemic.

Chapter 14

LA County Superior Court Appeal
For My Medical License Reinstatement

After receiving Judge Juárez' "Proposed Decision" to deny my petition for medical license reinstatement in the Administrative Law Court, (Appendix #377) I petitioned to the California Medical Board for a reconsideration of this judgment. (Appendix #378) I again argued that the original Decision was based on perjured testimony by the patient's daughter. I detailed how the LAC-USC Medical Administration had retaliated against me for my outspoken criticisms of the pain and symptom management of terminally ill cancer and AIDS patients.

I also argued that my research and publications on anticoagulation constituted rehabilitation and that my challenges to anticoagulation guidelines for VTE were unrebutted by any medical expert in the hearing.

The Board denied my petition without comment.

The next step in my battle with the California Medical Board was to submit a "Writ of Administrative Mandamus" to LA County Superior Court appealing the denial of license reinstatement. (Appendix #382) In this document, I basically made the same arguments as in the petition to the California Medical Board for reconsideration of the Decision. Deputy Attorney General McKay responded with a "Return by Way of Answer to Verified Petition for Writ of Administrative Mandate." (Appendix #392) This document concluded:

WHEREFORE, Respondent prays:

a) The Petition for a writ of mandate be denied;
b) Petitioner take nothing in this action;
c) Respondent be granted its costs;
d) A statement of decision be rendered; and

e)   Respondent be granted such other and further relief as this court deems proper.

My lawyer friends told me that the legal doctrine of "Res Judicata" meant that is was useless to try to relitigate the original unjust decision to revoke my license. However, my medical journal articles challenging the use of anticoagulants in VTE could be a completely different basis for an appeal the denial of license reinstatement. I needed a strategy to bring attention to those articles, the catastrophic harm caused by anticoagulants for VTE, and to my case. Doing so could be a way to trump the biased medical malpractice court system, the California Medical Board, and its representative Deputy AG McKay.

Contacting Leaders of the U.S. Department of Health and Human Services (HHS)

Shortly after the article challenging the evidence-basis of VTE prophylaxis and treatment and recommending trials comparing diet with standard anticoagulants (Chapter 13) appeared (http://www.tbiomed.com/content/7/1/31), I sent emails to about 20 leaders at the Food and Drug Administration (FDA) and National Institutes of Health (NIH). The email that I sent to Janet Woodcock, MD, Director of the Center for Drug Research and Evaluation of the FDA, was representative: (Appendix #398)

> From: David Cundiff
> Sent: Aug 12, 2010 06:49:50 PM
> To: Janet Woodcock, MD
> Subject: Venous thromboembolism: Will diet work as well or better than anticoagulants?
>
> Dear Dr. Woodcock,
>
> Yesterday, the BioMed Central Journal *Theoretical Biology and Medicine Modelling* published my review of anticoagulants and diet for VTE that concluded by proposing randomized non-inferiority trials to compare standard anticoagulants with low VTE risk

diets for both prophylaxis and treatment of VTE:
http://www.tbiomed.com/content/7/1/31

Your expert opinion about the advisability of the NIH
and/or NICE sponsoring RCTs to compare standard
anticoagulants and low VTE risk diets for prophylaxis
and treatment of VTE would be appreciated. A
"readers comments" link is at the right on the front
page.

Thank you.
Best wishes,
David K. Cundiff, MD

Dr. Woodcock designated Ann Farrell, MD, Acting Director of
the Division of Hematology Products, to respond to my email
requesting a critique of my article. Dr. Farrell was explicit about
refusing to go on record with a critique of my paper: (Appendix #387)

We have reviewed your interesting paper but have no
written critique. Our suggestion would be that you
contact NIH and/or NICE directly to discuss funding
opportunities for your proposed randomized,
controlled trials comparing standard anticoagulants
with diet for prophylaxis and treatment of venous
thromboembolism. . . .

I took Dr. Farrell's suggestion and directed my next email to
Francis Collins, MD, Director of the NIH. To hopefully get his
attention, I used the subject heading, "Dr. Janet Woodcock referred
me to you about anticoagulants for venous thromboembolism." To
try to ensure that my email would not be ignored, I copied the
following Department of Health and Human Services leaders:

Janet Woodcock, MD, Director of Center for Drug
Evaluation and Research in the FDA
Margaret Hamburg, MD, FDA Commissioner
Donald Berwick, MD, Director of Center for Medicare
and Medicaid Services

161

Susan Shurin, MD, Acting Director National Heart, Lung, and Blood Institute

Ann T. Farrell, MD, Center for Drug Evaluation and Research Hematology Products Director

Carolyn Clancy, MD, Agency for Healthcare Research and Quality

Kathleen Sebelius, Secretary of Health and Human Services (HHS)

My email to Dr. Collins began: (Appendix #395)

> I am the lead author of an article published in a BioMed Central Journal that provided literature documentation that anticoagulant prophylaxis and treatment for venous thromboembolism (VTE) unnecessarily causes about 40,000 bleeding and rebound clotting deaths per year worldwide, about 20,000 of which occur in the U.S. http://www.tbiomed.com/content/7/1/31 . . .

A month later, Susan Shurin, MD, Acting Director of the National Heart, Lung, and Blood Institute, replied for Dr. Collins. Her email concluded: (Appendix #396)

> The risks and benefits of the prophylactic and therapeutic use of current anticoagulation therapies are well recognized. Therefore, the NHLBI actively supports basic, translational, and clinical research on safer and more effective therapeutic options for VTE.

> To be selected for National Institutes of Health funding, the clinical research applications undergo intensive peer-review process. This system is established in order to select the most important, feasible, and well-designed studies. Should you submit an application for a study comparing diet with standard anticoagulants, it will be similarly reviewed for its impact and feasibility.

Just as the FDA had declined to critique my article, Dr. Shurin, representing the NIH, sidestepped a detailed, transparent analysis of my data showing that anticoagulants for VTE do catastrophic harm.

Faced with FDA and NIH stonewalling and avoiding a direct response to my evidence that drugs they were regulating were killing tens of thousands of Americans each year, I forwarded Dr. Shurin's email to dozens of researchers that conducted trials on anticoagulant drugs. My boilerplate email read:

> I emailed Dr. Francis Collins, NIH Chief, and some others involved in allocating research grants at the NIH about the recent low VTE risk diet for VTE randomized trial proposal. Their response is below (i.e., Dr. Shurin's email response for Dr. Collins). I think that it is fair to say that a diet versus standard anticoagulant VTE prophylaxis or treatment trial proposal from you would receive serious consideration.
>
> I do hope that you might be interested in applying for an NIH grant for a trial. . . .

Only two anticoagulation researchers responded to my email. They both indicated that they might participate in a randomized trial of diet versus anticoagulants for VTE if the NIH asked them to do it and funded the study, but they wouldn't go to the trouble of writing a protocol for an NIH grant, submitting it, and taking the chance that it wouldn't be funded. While these invitations from the FDA and NIH to submit trial protocols seemed responsive to my emails, they appeared to avoid bringing the public's attention to the dangers of anticoagulants with a paper trail that they calculated would avert a scandal if the medical profession and public later found out that they knowingly failed to protect the public.

I worried that Department of Health and Human Services scientific leaders, for whatever reasons, were choosing to protect the financial interests of drug companies and medical special interests over safeguarding the health of the public.

Correspondence with HHS leaders from the FDA and NIH

In preparation for my Superior Court appeal on January 25, 2011, I emailed NIH Director Dr. Francis Collins asking for a letter of support. (Appendix #384) My email began:

> I write to ask your help with a letter of support in my appeal to LA County Superior Court on January 25, 2011 of an Administrative Law Court's decision to deny the reinstatement of my medical license. My case relates to the NIH because my case hangs on anticoagulant therapy being the standard of care in the U.S., trumping my medical judgment as a physician and a researcher in anticoagulation medicine. I am board certified in hematology, oncology, and internal medicine.

I went on to lay out my case for stopping the anticoagulants in patient BR. I also mentioned my research and publications in anticoagulation medicine that justified my current position that I would not prescribe anticoagulants in a future patient.

Several weeks later, a representative of the NIH Office of General Council replied for Dr. Collins, informing me that NIH staff remain "neutral" in medico-legal proceedings and that I would receive no letter of support. I next emailed Dr. Susan Shurin asking for her to send me a declaration verifying my correspondence with her and Dr. Collins. I referenced the General Council's position prohibiting letters of support in legal cases and specified that the declaration I was requesting was not a letter of support. (Appendix #406)

The Executive Assistant to Dr. Collins responded for Dr. Shurin writing that Dr. Shurin could not give me a letter of support. (Appendix #388) To this further evidence of stonewalling by the NIH, I replied directly to Dr. Collins. My email began: (Appendix #400)

> The Office of General Counsel for the Department of Health and Human Services' decision to refuse to allow Dr. Susan Shurin to send me a declaration verifying my correspondence with you and her response on your behalf should be put in context.

My email to you on October 4, 2010 stated, ". . . anticoagulant prophylaxis and treatment for venous thromboembolism (VTE) unnecessarily causes about 40,000 bleeding and rebound clotting deaths per year worldwide, about 20,000 of which occur in the U.S." In writing to you, I brought to the attention of the NIH to my article, "Diet as prophylaxis and treatment for venous thromboembolism?" (http://www.tbiomed.com/content/7/1/31) Using the methods of evidence-based medicine, this paper reviews prophylaxis and treatment of VTE with anticoagulant medications and finds they do catastrophic harm to patients.

I concluded my email to Dr. Collins:

Dr. Collins, the data documenting the great harm of anticoagulant treatment and prophylaxis of VTE has been brought to your attention and the decision-makers of the FDA and NIH. You have the opportunity to uphold the mission of HHS to protect the public and be rightfully credited with performing your service to the public.

Whether my medical license is reinstated as a result of Dr. Shurin's declaration about our correspondence or not, I hope you choose to protect the public now.

Dr. Collins ignored my email.

Responding to Deputy Attorney General McKay's Brief

Having been unemployed for 13 years due to the loss of my medical license, I was in no position to hire an attorney to represent me in court. When I called the clerk of the LA County Superior Court to clarify the schedule of submission of briefs for the January 25, 2011 license reinstatement appeal, the clerk told me the deadline for my initial brief was January 10, 2011. To my shock, I found that my deadline was really January 3, 2011 because of the difference between "court days" and "calendar days." Deputy Attorney General McKay's "Opposing Brief" arrived on January 7, 2011, beginning with: (Appendix #401)

> Respondent has yet to receive any additional documents other than the original Writ. Since Respondent has been prejudiced by the failure of Petitioner to serve any additional authority or other evidence he might have filed with the Court but not served, Respondent requests that such authority and/or evidence not be considered.

Deputy AG McKay responded to my Petition for Reconsideration of the California Medical Board's Decision (Appendix #384) to adopt Judge Juárez' Proposed Decision to deny the reinstatement of my medical license and included this document as an exhibit in his opposing brief.

Deputy AG McKay also submitted for the court records my email to him on December 22, 2010, which began: (Appendix #402)

> Dr. Francis Collins, NIH Director, and the relevant staff at the NIH and FDA are copied in this email. I asked for Dr. Collins to write the judge in my support for the January 25, 2011 hearing on my medical license reinstatement . I realize that no witnesses may be called at the hearing, but written statements from experts may be submitted.

I concluded the email to Mr. McKay with a request that he find expert physicians to address my peer-reviewed medical journal articles supporting my position that I would not again prescribe anticoagulants for VTE:

> Besides Dr. Collins, I will be asking two other physicians to submit letters to the Court critiquing these articles in regard to the standard of care for venous thromboembolism (VTE) and my medical opinion that anticoagulants increase the risk of death

in the treatment of VTE. I request that, in the interest of justice, you consult with at least three physicians in internal medicine regarding whether the content of these articles can be a valid basis for my inconvenient opinion. Please have your chosen consultants also submit their letters to the Court in sufficient time so they may be considered by the Judge in the upcoming hearing.

Dr. Collins and his associates copied in this email are the top government regulators in the country of the practice of medicine. I request that you ask your medical consultants to call upon their expertise in the field of anticoagulation medicine in doing a thorough evaluation of my case before they write their letters for the Court.

In his opposing brief the next month, Deputy AG McKay did not call on expert physicians to address my medical journal articles.

Email Campaign to HHS Secretary Kathleen Sebelius

The NIH and FDA leaders continued to stonewall and refused to publicly critique my evidence from peer-reviewed medical journal articles about the ineffectiveness and dangers of anticoagulation treatment. In looking for a way to do their jobs and protect the public, I found that HHS was operating under an "Open Government" initiative, (http://www.hhs.gov/open/plan/opengovernmentplan/exsummary.html) as described on the HHS website:

An Open Government is one that is *transparent*, publishing government data that generates significant benefit for citizens and which helps the public hold the government accountable. An Open Government embraces the notion of public *participation* in the work of government. And it's one that is effective at encouraging *collaboration* across the government and with the world outside government. Above all, an

167

Open Government is one that works better—one that leverages the principles of transparency, participation, and collaboration to deliver better results to the American people.

I asked my friends to send emails to Secretary Kathleen Sebelius about anticoagulants referencing the "Open Government Plan" in the HHS:

Subject: David Cundiff's medical license reinstatement case
From: David Cundiff
To: List suppressed

Sent: Jan 13, 2011 07:29:15 AM

Dear Friends,

My medical license reinstatement case will hang on my correspondence with FDA and NIH physicians about my challenges to the standard medical guidelines for treating and preventing deep venous thrombosis and pulmonary emboli. The opposing brief [Appendix #402] of Deputy Attorney General Klint McKay and my brief [Appendix #403] both reference my emails to and from leaders in the Department of Health and Human Services (HHS). So far, HHS is stonewalling about analyzing the medical journal article (http://www.tbiomed.com/content/7/1/31) I sent them.

Please send the following email letter with any of your edits to the Secretary of HHS, Kathleen Sebelius and CC Dr. Francis Collins, Director of the National Institutes of Health.

Thanks for your help.
Best wishes,
David

Below is the template for the campaign to prompt a critique of anticoagulation prophylaxis and treatment for VTE:

> Subject: HHS transparency and accountability regarding venous thromboembolism prophylaxis and treatment
>
> To: HHS Secretary Kathleen Sebelius
> CC: Francis Collins, MD, NIH Director
>
> Dear Secretary Sebelius,
>
> In conjunction with the "HHS Open Government Plan," I request that you ask NIH Director Dr. Francis Collins to order the publication on the HHS website of the analysis of NIH and FDA scientists regarding the evidence-basis of anticoagulation prophylaxis and treatment for venous thromboembolism. A recent medical journal article (http://www.tbiomed.com/content/7/1/31) suggests that anticoagulants do net harm for patients in regard to venous thromboembolism and are responsible for up to 20,000 unnecessary deaths in the U.S. per year. This issue calls for an official, detailed, transparent response.
>
> Thank you.
> Sincerely,

At least 20 of my friends sent emails to Secretary Sebelius. A few received boiler-plate automated replies that generally supported a range of HHS' policies not related to the query. The Secretary's website indicated that responses to the sender's issue would be forthcoming later.

Email to HHS Leadership Inviting a Declaration for My Appeal Hearing

On January 20, 2011, five days before the Superior Court Hearing for my license reinstatement, I sent an email to Dr. Francis Collins, NIH Director and Margaret Hamburg, MD, Commissioner of the FDA inviting their input in my case. (Appendix #408) FDA and NIH leaders and medical media journalists were also copied. The email began:

> A hearing will be held on January 25, 2011, in Los Angeles County Superior Court, with much more at stake than the reinstatement of my medical license. The lives of tens of thousands of Americans who die each year from complications of anticoagulant drugs will be at stake along with the reputation of the HHS for openness, transparency, and commitment to evidence-based medicine.

After again laying out the issues involved in anticoagulation for VTE, I concluded:

> Protecting the health of all Americans is the duty of the HHS. If Deputy AG McKay is right, that my opinion that anticoagulant treatment for VTE is harmful to the public, it is your obligation to use the authority and credibility of the HHS as the country's primary health care regulator to help Deputy AG McKay defeat me in court.
>
> Should you find it in the best interest of the public, you are invited to testify by means of a declaration on Deputy AG McKay's behalf in support of the opposition to returning my medical license. While the Superior Court rules and procedures may not allow further declarations to be submitted at this point, I will ask the judge to admit into evidence any declaration representing the HHS that you wish to send to Deputy AG McKay.

In accordance with the HHS "Open Government Plan," I request your response to this issue in your regulatory role as protector of the health of Americans.

No one in HHS responded.

License Reinstatement Hearing Continuation Decision by the Judge

Judge James C. Chalfant presided on January 25, 2011 in the Los Angeles Superior Court for my medical license reinstatement hearing. After Deputy AG McKay and I were called and identified ourselves, Judge Chalfant said, "This case is a mess." He was referring to my late Opening Brief, followed on the same day by Deputy AG McKay's Opposition Brief, and subsequently my Reply to his Opposition. My exhibits from the administrative law hearing were also out of order.

In my defense for submitting the late initial brief, I told the Judge that I had called the court clerk to clarify the schedule for the briefs. The court clerk told me that January 10, 2011 was my deadline for the opening brief. The relevant statute that Deputy AG McKay referred me to stated that the opening brief was due 15 court days before the hearing. The clerk's affirmation of my calculation of January 10th as the deadline date mistakenly substituted "calendar days" for "court days," leading to my late Opening Brief.

Judge Chalfant said that the court rules and regulations would permit him to deny my appeal because of the late brief. However, indicating that he wanted to hear what was at issue in my appeal, he chose to reschedule the hearing for May 27, 2011.

I was delighted at the opportunity to have four more months to prepare my case, flush out a critique of my medical journal articles by the FDA and NIH leaders, and try to facilitate game-changing attention to the case by publishing this book.

Efforts to Generate HHS Responses to My Medical Journal Articles

On February 22, 2011, Dr. George Lundberg forwarded to me an email from the office of Dr. Susan Shurin, Acting Heart, Lung, and Blood

Institute Director. Dr. Lundberg's request on my behalf to the NIH concluded: (Appendix #409)

> Please analyze the recent medical journal article (http://www.tbiomed.com/content/7/1/31) which suggests that anticoagulants do net harm for patients in regard to venous thromboembolism and are responsible for up to 20,000 unnecessary deaths in the U.S. per year. This issue calls for an official, detailed, transparent response. Many American (and other) lives hang in the balance. This is obvious pragmatic "Comparative Effectiveness Research" in action.

Representing the NIH, Dr. Susan Shurin's reply to Dr. Lundberg's request for a critique of my challenges to anticoagulation for VTE was just as unresponsive to his request as she had been before to me. Rather than responding to the claim that anticoagulant drugs unnecessarily kill 40,000 per a year, she completely sidestepped the issue: (Appendix #410)

> ...The scientific community recognizes the risks and benefits of anticoagulation therapy and is engaged in analysis and discussion of the optimal treatment and prophylaxis of patients at high risk for VTE.

The brief cover note that came to me from Dr. Lundberg relating to this correspondence said,

> David,
> Here is the NIH response. They decline to recognize the problem.
> george

In response to Dr. Shurin's letter to Dr. Lundberg, I sent an email to Dr. Shurin, Deputy AG Klint McKay, and medical journalists Shannon Brownlee and Jeanne Lenzer. Referring to the Obama Administration "Open Government " initiative obliging the U.S. Department of Health and Human Services to cooperate with outside scientists and the public in improving health care, the subject line read, "NIH non-responsiveness to inquiries violates "HHS Open Government Plan." Copies of the email went to FDA and NIH leaders and others. Addressing Dr. Shurin's non-responsive reply to Dr. Lundberg, I wrote: (Appendix #411)

> Dr. Shurin, given the body of evidence challenging anticoagulation prophylaxis and treatment of venous thromboembolism presented to you in my article that Dr. Lundberg cited and articles referenced in that paper, your reply was not responsive to his request. Your non-responsiveness is not in accordance with the "HHS Open Government Plan." Using the methodology of evidence-based medicine with data derived from the medical literature, this article documents that up to 20,000 Americans die unnecessarily per year from complications of anticoagulant prophylaxis and treatment for VTE. Dr. Lundberg referred you to that article and requested your "official, detailed, transparent response." As the designated representative of the primary entity charged with safeguarding the health and safety of the American public, your duty in furthering the mission of the U.S. Department of Health and Human Services and complying with its policies is to be responsive to public inquiries. Please either issue an official, detailed, transparent analysis of the paper or publicly acknowledge the refusal of HHS to do so.

Neither Dr. Shurin nor any other HHS leader issued a reply.

Legal Briefs in Preparation for the May 27, 2011 License Hearing

Presiding Judge James C. Chalfant of the LA County Superior Court announced that my "Opening Brief" in the medical license reinstatement appeal hearing would be due by March 24, 2011. With help from my copyeditor Michelle Fergus, a former legal secretary, and Travers Wood, an attorney friend, I wrote the 15 page brief. (Appendix #412) Six exhibits supported the points in my brief.

(Appendices #413, #414, #415, #416, #417, and #418) The essence of the conclusion of the Opening Brief was the following:

> Petitioner's medical judgment that anticoagulants for VTE treatment increase the risk of death has not been rebutted by readers of his six peer-reviewed medical articles published from 2004 – 2010. That anticoagulants cause catastrophic harm to patients has not been rebutted by the FDA or NIH leaders in charge of regulating these drugs that have also read these articles.

> The burden is on Respondent to produce two or more declarations by authoritative physicians to address Petitioner's medical judgment in 2011 that anticoagulant medication for treatment of VTE increases the risk of death.

> Failing to produce compelling sworn declarations from Respondent's physician experts showing that omitting anticoagulant drugs in treating VTE patients increases the risk of death, Respondent should reinstate Petitioner's medical license.

Deputy AG McKay's opposition brief is due on April 21, 2011 and my reply is due May 12, 2011.

A Discover Magazine Article Referenced My Cochrane VTE Review

Medical Journalists Shannon Brownlee and Jeanne Lenzer specialize in articles about ineffective and dangerous medical treatments and financial conflicts of interest among researchers. Ms. Brownlee's book, *Overtreated*, about unnecessary and harmful tests and treatments, was quite successful. They had expressed some interest in my challenges to the evidence-basis of anticoagulation. However, they had other writing priorities and couldn't devote the time to research and investigate the extreme complexities of anticoagulation medicine.

In November 2010, they co-authored an article in Discover Magazine entitled, *The Problem With Medicine: We Don't Know If Most of It Works*.[1] In that article, they made reference to my Cochrane review of anticoagulants for venous thrombosis.[2] They referenced my Cochrane review to suggest that an anti-inflammatory drug like ibuprofen may be as effective as anticoagulants for VTE.

Carol Newell, a woman who had been treated with anticoagulants for pulmonary emboli, read the Discovery Magazine article and emailed the Cochrane Collaboration for more information. Since I was the lead author of the review in question, the Cochrane volunteer managing correspondence copied me in her reply to Ms. Newell's email. (Appendix #419) Ms. Newell had been concerned about minor bleeding during her four month course of treatment with Coumadin and about the possibility of developing another episode of pulmonary emboli requiring more anticoagulants. She had questioned her doctor about alternatives to anticoagulants.

My dilemma in answering Ms. Newell about alternatives to anticoagulants to treat VTE was that my views are discredited because my medical license is revoked. And the medical establishment has ignored my multiple medical journal articles challenging the evidence-basis of anticoagulants for VTE. Consequently, giving her my opinion that anticoagulants do harm for VTE patients might only confuse and worry her. On the other hand, if our correspondence might be shared with Dr. David Tovey, Chief Editor of the Cochrane Collaboration, and the leaders of the FDA and NIH, they might be moved to respond by producing critiques of my articles.

Without initially responding to Ms. Newell's questions about VTE treatment, I sent her an email explaining the non-responsiveness of the medical establishment to my challenges to anticoagulant treatment of VTE and asked for her permission to share our correspondence with all the stakeholders in the controversy. (Appendix #420) She agreed to share our correspondence with FDA and NIH leaders and other anticoagulation medicine stakeholders, so I responded in detail to her question. I concluded with the following: (Appendix #421)

> I will copy the relevant HHS leaders with this email
> and see if they give you, me, and the world a detailed
> and transparent analysis of the evidence I presented to

175

them. As you can see, an authoritative and definitive answer to your question is possible, but it cannot come from me. Only HHS Secretary Kathleen Sebelius and the top health regulators in the NIH and FDA can answer your question.

Ms. Newell and I are still waiting for responses from the HHS and Cochrane.

Institute of Medicine Report on "Trustworthiness" of Medical Guidelines

On March 23, 2011, my email inbox contained a medical news email from the AMA. It included a notice about the Institute of Medicine releasing a report entitled, *Standards for Developing Trustworthy Clinical Practice Guidelines* (CPGs).[3] Of great significance to my case, this report changed the definition of "clinical practice guideline." The preceding Institute of Medicine definition of CPG was, "systematically developed statements to assist practitioner and patient decisions about appropriate health care for specific clinical circumstances." The new definition became, "statements that include recommendations intended to optimize patient care that are informed by a systematic review of evidence and an assessment of benefits and harms of alternative care options."

The CPG that I supposedly violated was implemented over the 1940s and 1950s, long before "systematic reviews of evidence" and rigorous "assessments of benefits and harms of alternative care options" existed in the medical literature. The now 50+ year old guideline calling for anticoagulant treatment of patients with venous thromboembolism would be allowed under the old definition of CPGs. A "systematically developed statement" does not address whether the statement is based on a consensus of expert opinion leaders (i.e., consensus-based) or is "evidence-based." However, the new terminology, "a systematic review of evidence and an assessment of benefits and harms of alternative care options," connotes that CPGs must now be evidence-based and must consider alternative options. The CPG requiring anticoagulant treatment of VTE was never based on a systematic review of evidence nor did it consider non drug options. By the new definition of CPG, the guideline to treat people with VTE with anticoagulants is not a valid guideline.

In all of the medical literature, there are only two articles giving systematic reviews of the evidence about anticoagulant treatment of venous thromboembolism. I authored one in Medscape General Medicine (http://www.medscape.com/viewarticle/487577) and co-authored the other with the Cochrane Collaboration (http://www.mrw.interscience.wiley.com/cochrane/clsysrev/articles/CD003746/frame.html). At my Administrative Law Hearing, Judge Juárez admitted these systematic reviews into evidence. I also co-authored the only review of diet as a non drug alternative to anticoagulants and concluded that a low VTE risk diet is likely to be beneficial and would not be harmful. (Appendix #397)

In an email to Deputy AG McKay, I asked him to have his medical consultants address whether the government's changed definition of CPG invalidated the anticoagulation for VTE guideline. (Appendix #422) On April 24, 2011, when Mr. McKay sends me his opposing brief, I will find out if he hired medical consultants and, if so, what they thought about the validity of the anticoagulation for VTE guideline under the new Institute of Medicine CPG and about my medical journal articles challenging the 50+ year old guideline.

Conclusion

After all the trials and tribulations of the past 32 years of this ordeal, I feel grateful that I undertook the practice of medicine. I enjoyed my years of practicing clinical medicine and teaching physicians in training despite the hostile work environment of the LA County + USC Medical Center. I do not blame the administrators of LAC-USC because the financial imperatives of a profoundly dysfunctional health care system propelled their actions.

I am privileged to be in a position to possibly help stop a terrible iatrogenic epidemic of anticoagulation-related deaths. Whether I win or lose in the May 27, 2011 LA County Superior Court hearing, I will continue to advocate for stopping the use of anticoagulants. Anticoagulant use is representative of the pervasiveness of biased research and financial conflicts of interest in modern western medicine. While a dysfunctional system of Medicaid funding directly led to my toxic work environment and my malpractice case, medical insurance from Medicare, Veterans Health Care System, and private insurance companies also get in the way of the optimal practice of medicine.

My ordeal also calls for a reanalysis of our medico-legal system that depends on decisions of non-medically trained judges informed by witnesses paid by the prosecution and defense to advocate for their positions. In my case, the California Medical Board responded to political and economic pressure and disregarded the medical circumstances involved in the revocation of my license. I have no idea if they paid any attention to my case other than signing off on the Proposed Decisions of judges.

"Sham peer-review," as in my case, has become an increasing problem in stifling health care innovation, efficiency, and quality of care improvement. Whistleblowing physicians who point out deficiencies in health care and expert physicians who pose competitive threats to local medical establishments may be targeted for retaliation like I was. Resolving the current medico-legal mess regarding physician malpractice requires a comprehensive overhaul of the tort system in health care.

While there are many goals in writing this book, three are most important:

- stop the epidemic of deaths and injuries from the use of anticoagulant drugs,
- improve the pain and symptom control of cancer and AIDS patients, and
- change the Medicaid reimbursement system for the LA County Department of Health Services and other places where it fosters inefficiencies and poor medical care.

The first step in achieving these goals is to have my medical license reinstated as a result of the Superior Court hearing on May 27, 2011.

Appendices

To access any appendix or exhibit online, go to
http://TheHealthEconomy.com/WD/Appendices.htm and click on the
appropriate appendix or exhibit.

Appendices

Appendices

185

Appendices

Appendices

Appendices

Appendices

Exhibits for Petition for Medical License Reinstatement (Chapter 12)

Exhibit 31—Letter from Attorney Richard Reinjohn to me 4-11-00

Exhibit 32—Letter from attorney Richard Reinjohn to me 5-31-00

Exhibit 33—Testimonial letter from Beverly Stender to Ronald Kauffman, MD 10-12-95

Exhibit 34—Testimonial letter from James A. Way to Supervisor Gloria Molino 11-14-94

Exhibit 35—Testimonial letter from James A. Way to me

Exhibit 36—Testimonial letter from Illona Heyen to Dr. John Bethune 12-9-87

Exhibit 37—Dr. Bethune responding to Ms. Heyen December 28, 1987

Exhibit 38—Testimonial letter from Luella Downs, RN to Maxine Patrick, RN 10-16-92

Exhibit 39—Testimonial letter from psychiatry resident Theron C. Wells, MD

Exhibit 40—Letter from Joseph H. Hafkenschiel re my nomination for CAHSAH physician of the year award 6-28-93

Exhibit 41—Thank you letter from Alice Nassimian, RN for my teaching nurses about pain management 10-20-94

Exhibit 42—Evergreen Hospital Medical Center pain management lecture evaluation summary 10-31-97

Exhibit 43—Pain management lecture to oncology nurses: Evaluation questionnaire summary 8-4-94

Exhibit 44—Letter from Maxine Patrick, RN to DHS Director Robert Gates regarding Pain and Palliative Care Service 3-12-93

References

Chapter 6

1. Hospital Annual Financial Data Archive. Office of Statewide Planning and Development. Available at: http://www.oshpd.cahwnet.gov/HQAD/HIRC/hospital/finance/annual_data/archive/index.htm, 2002.

Chapter 7

1. Alan Abrahamson, Miles Corwin. Man Kills Self as City Watches. LA Times. http://articles.latimes.com/1998/may/01/news/mn-45260. May 01, 1998.
2. Cundiff DK, Manyemba J, Pezzullo JC: Anticoagulants versus non-steroidal anti-inflammatories or placebo for treatment of venous thromboembolism. The Cochrane Database of Systematic Reviews 2006, Issue 1. Art. No.: CD003746. DOI: 10.1002/14651858.CD003746.pub2. http://www.mrw.interscience.wiley.com/cochrane/clsysrev/articles/CD003746/frame.html.

Chapter 8

1. Yi M. Doctor found reckless for not relieving pain - $1.5 million jury verdict for family of cancer patient who went home to Hayward to die. San Francisco Chronicle. http://www.sfgate.com/cgi-bin/article.cgi?file=/chronicle/archive/2001/06/14/MN207007.DTL. June 14, 2001.

Chapter 9

1. Yi M. Doctor found reckless for not relieving pain - $1.5 million jury verdict for family of cancer patient who went home to Hayward to die. San Francisco Chronicle. http://www.sfgate.com/cgi-bin/article.cgi?file=/chronicle/archive/2001/06/14/MN207007.DTL. June 14, 2001.

Chapter 11

1. Cundiff DK: Clinical Evidence For Rebound Hypercoagulability After Discontinuing Oral Anticoagulants For Venous Thromboembolism. Medscape Journal of Medicine 2008, 10(11):258 http://www.medscape.com/viewarticle/582408.
2. Goldhaber S, Dunn K, MacDougall R: New onset of venous thromboembolism among hospitalized patients at Brigham and Women's Hospital is caused more often by prophylaxis failure than by withholding treatment. Chest 2000, 118:1680-1684. http://chestjournal.chestpubs.org/content/118/6/1680.full.pdf

Chapter 13

1. Nielsen HK, Husted SE, Krusell LR, Fasting H, Charles P, Hansen HH: Silent pulmonary embolism in patients with deep venous thrombosis. Incidence and fate in a randomized, controlled trial of anticoagulation versus no anticoagulation. Journal of Internal Medicine 1994, 235(5):457-461.

2. Nielsen HK, Husted SE, Krusell LR, Fasting H, Charles P, Hansen HH, Nielsen BO, Petersen JB, Bechgaard P: Anticoagulant therapy in deep venous thrombosis. A randomized controlled study. Thrombosis Research 1994, 73(3-4):215-226.

3. Hyers TM, Hull RD, Weg JG: Antithrombotic therapy for venous thromboembolic disease. Chest 1986, 89(2 Suppl):26S-35S.

4. Hyers TM, Hull RD, Weg JG: Antithrombotic therapy for venous thromboembolic disease. Chest 1989, 95(2 Suppl):37S-51S.

5. Hyers TM, Hull RD, Weg JG: Antithrombotic therapy for venous thromboembolic disease. Chest 1992, 102(4 Suppl):408S-425S.

6. Hyers TM, Hull RD, Weg JG: Antithrombotic Therapy for Venous Thromboembolic Disease. Chest 1995, 108(4):335S-351S.

7. Hyers TM, Agnelli G, Hull RD, Weg JG, Morris TA, Samama M, Tapson V: Antithrombotic therapy for venous thromboembolic disease. Chest 1998, 114(5 Suppl):561S-578S.
   http://www.chestjournal.org/cgi/reprint/114/5/561S.pdf

8. Hyers TM, Agnelli G, Hull RD, Morris TA, Samama M, Tapson V, Weg JG: Antithrombotic Therapy for Venous Thromboembolic Disease. Chest 2001, 119(1 Suppl):176S-193S.
   http://www.chestjournal.org/cgi/content/full/119/1_suppl/176S?ijkey=736b45ffd56f0c4b06a2c78a22dd3147bb98ec49&keytype2=tf_ipsecsha

9. Cundiff DK: Anticoagulation Therapy for Venous Thromboembolism. MedGenMed 2004, 6(3): http://www.medscape.com/viewarticle/487577.

10. Financial Disclosures. Chest, 126(3_suppl):167S-171.
    http://www.chestjournal.org/cgi/content/full/126/163_suppl/167S.
    http://www.chestjournal.org/cgi/content/full/126/3_suppl/167S

11. The Seventh ACCP Conference on Antithrombotic and Thrombolytic Therapy: Evidence-Based Guidelines. CHEST vol. 126 no. September 2004, 126(3 suppl):167S-171S
    http://chestjournal.chestpubs.org/content/126/163_suppl/167S.full.pdf+html.

12. The Seventh ACCP Conference on Antithrombotic and Thrombolytic Therapy: Evidence-Based Guidelines, Financial Disclosures, Supplement Sponsorship. CHEST September 2004, 126(no. 3 suppl): 167S-171S
    http://chestjournal.chestpubs.org/content/126/163_suppl/167S/suppl/DC161.

References

13. Geerts WH, Bergqvist D, Pineo GF, Heit JA, Samama CM, Lassen MR, Colwell CW: Prevention of venous thromboembolism. Chest 2008, 133(6 suppl):381S-453S.
http://chestjournal.chestpubs.org/content/133/6_suppl/381S.full

14. Goldhaber S, Dunn K, MacDougall R: New onset of venous thromboembolism among hospitalized patients at Brigham and Women's Hospital is caused more often by prophylaxis failure than by withholding treatment. Chest 2000, 118:1680-1684.
http://chestjournal.chestpubs.org/content/118/6/1680.full.pdf

15. Cundiff DK: Reply to letters re: Anticoagulation therapy for venous thromboembolism. Med Gen Med 2005, 6(4):http://www.medscape.com/viewarticle/496149.
http://www.medscape.com/viewarticle/496149

16. Ridker PM, Goldhaber SZ, Danielson E, Rosenberg Y, Eby CS, Deitcher SR, Cushman M, Moll S, Kessler CM, Elliott CG, Paulson R, Wong T, Bauer KA, Schwartz BA, Miletich JP, Bounameaux H, Glynn RJ, the PREVENT Investigators: Long-Term, Low-Intensity Warfarin Therapy for the Prevention of Recurrent Venous Thromboembolism. N Engl J Med February 24, 2003, 348(15):1425-1434. Available at:
http://content.nejm.org/cgi/content/abstract/1348/1415/1425.

17. Cundiff DK: Commentary - Insufficient Evidence Supporting Low-Intensity Warfarin for Venous Thromboembolism (VTE) Prophylaxis. Medscape General Medicine™,
http://www.medscape.com/viewarticle/457570.

18. Kakkar VV, Flanc C, O'Shea M, Flute P, Howe CT, Clarke MB: Treatment of deep-vein thrombosis--a random trial. Br J Surg 1968, 55(11):858.

19. Ott P, Eldrup E, Oxholm P: The value of anticoagulant therapy in deep venous thrombosis in the lower limbs in elderly, mobilized patients. A double-blind, placebo-controlled investigation with open therapeutic guidance. Ugeskr Laeger 1988, 150:218-221.

20. Cundiff D, Manyemba J, Pezzullo J: Anticoagulants versus non-steroidal anti-inflammatories or placebo for treatment of venous thromboembolism. The Cochrane Database of Systematic Reviews 2006, (Issue 1):Art. No.: CD003746. DOI: 003710.001002/14651858.CD14003746.pub14651852.
http://www.mrw.interscience.wiley.com/cochrane/clsysrev/articles/CD003746/frame.html

21. Lundberg GD: Is the Current Standard of Medical Practice for Treating Venous Thromboembolism Simply Wrong? Medscape General Medicine., 6(3):http://www.medscape.com/viewarticle/488717.

22. Cundiff DK: Letters to Editor re Anticoagulation Therapy for Venous Thromboembolism. Medscape General Medicine., 6(4):http://www.medscape.com/viewarticle/496148.
http://www.medscape.com/viewarticle/487577

23. Stein PD, Alpert JS, Bussey HI, Dalen JE, Turpie AGG: Antithrombotic Therapy in Patients With Mechanical and Biological Prosthetic Heart Valves. Chest 2001, 119(90010):220S-227.
http://www.chestjournal.org/cgi/content/full/119/1_suppl/220S#T1

24. Hylek EM, Evans-Molina C, Shea C, Henault LE, Regan S: Major Hemorrhage and Tolerability of Warfarin in the First Year of Therapy Among Elderly Patients With Atrial Fibrillation.
10.1161/CIRCULATIONAHA.106.653048. Circulation, 115(21):2689-2696.
http://circ.ahajournals.org/cgi/content/abstract/115/21/2689

25. Go AS, Hylek EM, Phillips KA: Prevalence of diagnosed atrial fibrillation in adults. National implications for rhythm management and stroke prevention: The Anticoagulation and Risk Factors in Atrial Fibrillation (ATRIA) study. JAMA 2001, 285:2370–2375.

26. Fang MC, Stafford RS, Ruskin JN, Singer DE: National Trends in Antiarrhythmic and Antithrombotic Medication Use in Atrial Fibrillation. Arch Intern Med 2004, 164(1):55-60. http://archinte.ama-assn.org/cgi/content/abstract/164/1/55

27. Singer DE, Albers GW, Dalen JE, Fang MC, Go AS, Halperin JL, Lip GYH, Manning WJ: Antithrombotic Therapy in Atrial Fibrillation. Chest 2008, 133(6 suppl):546S-592S.
http://chestjournal.chestpubs.org/content/133/6_suppl/546S.abstract

28. Lip GYH, Agnelli G, Thach AA, Knight E, Roste D, Tangelderf MJD: Oral anticoagulation in atrial fibrillation: A pan-European patient survey. European Journal of Internal Medicine 2007, 18(3):202-208.

29. Cundiff DK: Anticoagulants for Non Valvular Atrial Fibrillation (NVAF) - Drug Review. Medscape General Medicine. 2003, Available at: http://www.medscape.com/viewarticle/448817 . Accessed February 26, 2003.

30. Flaherty ML, Kissela B, Woo D, Kleindorfer D, Alwell K, Sekar P, Moomaw CJ, Haverbusch M, Broderick JP: The increasing incidence of anticoagulant-associated intracerebral hemorrhage. Neurology 2007, 68(2):116-121. http://www.neurology.org/cgi/content/abstract/68/2/116

31. Flaherty M: Anticoagulant-associated intracerebral hemorrhage. Semin Neurol. 2010 Nov, 30(5):565-572.

32. Walker AM, Bennett D,: Epidemiology and outcomes in patients with atrial fibrillation in the United States. Heart Rhythm. 2008, 5(10):1365-1372.

33. Taylor FC, Cohen H, Ebrahim S: Systematic review of long term anticoagulation or antiplatelet treatment in patients with non-rheumatic atrial fibrillation. BMJ 2001, 322:321-326.
http://bmj.com/cgi/content/full/322/7282/321?maxtoshow=&HITS=10&hits=10&RESULTFORMAT=&author1=taylor%2C+f&searchid=10355253

References

51878_25602&stored_search=&FIRSTINDEX=0&resourcetype=1,2,3,4,1 0

34. Geerts WH, Pineo GF, Heit JA, Bergqvist D, Lassen MR, Colwell CW, Ray JG: Prevention of Venous Thromboembolism: The Seventh ACCP Conference on Antithrombotic and Thrombolytic Therapy. Chest 2004, 126(3_suppl):338S-400. C:\Documents and Settings\David K. Cundiff\My Documents\Whistle\DVT\Chest AC Guidelines 9-04\Prevention of VTE Geerts.htm

35. Chimowitz MI, Lynn MJ, Howlett-Smith H, Stern BJ, Hertzberg VS, Frankel MR, Levine SR, Chaturvedi S, Kasner SE, Benesch CG, Sila CA, Jovin TG, Romano JG, (WASID) tW-ASIDTI: Comparison of Warfarin and Aspirin for Symptomatic Intracranial Arterial Stenosis. N Engl J Med 2005, 352(13):1305-1316. http://content.nejm.org/cgi/content/abstract/352/13/1305

36. Martí-Fàbregas J, Cocho D, Martí-Vilalta JL, Gich I, Belvís R, Bravo Y, M M, Castellanos M, Rodríguez-Campello A, Egido J, Geffner D, Gil-Núñez A, Marta J, Navarro R, Obach V, E. P: Aspirin or anticoagulants in stenosis of the middle cerebral artery: A randomized trial. Cerebrovasc Dis 2006, 22(2-3):162-169.

37. The ESPRIT Study Group, Algra A: Medium intensity oral anticoagulants versus aspirin after cerebral ischaemia of arterial origin (ESPRIT): a randomised controlled trial. Lancet Neurol. 2007, 6(2):115-124.

38. Anand SS, Bates S, Ginsberg JS, Levine M, Buller H, Prins M, Haley S, Kearon C, Hirsh J, Gent M: Recurrent venous thrombosis and heparin therapy: an evaluation of the importance of early activated partial thromboplastin times. Archives of Internal Medicine 1999, 159(17):2029-2032.

39. Cundiff DK: Clinical evidence for rebound hypercoagulability after discontinuing oral anticoagulants for venous thromboembolism. Medscape J Med 2008, 10(11):258 http://www.medscape.com/viewarticle/582408.

40. Collins R, MacMahon S, Flather M, Baigent C, Remvig L, Mortensen S, Appleby P, Godwin J, Yusuf S, Peto R: Clinical effects of anticoagulant therapy in suspected acute myocardial infarction: systematic overview of randomised trials. BMJ 1996, 313(7058):652-659.

41. Cairns JA, Theroux P, Lewis HD, Jr., Ezekowitz M, Meade TW: Antithrombotic Agents in Coronary Artery Disease. Chest 2001, 119(90010):228S-252S. http://www.chestjournal.org

42. Altman LK. Sharon, Gravely Ill, Invited the Public Inside. NY Times. http://www.nytimes.com/2006/02/28/health/28docs.html?pagewanted=all. February 28, 2006.

43. Altman LK. The Doctor's World - As in Sharon's Case, Handling of Stroke Has Many Variables. Ny Times. January 17, 2006.

207

44. Albers GW, Amarenco P, Easton JD, Sacco RL, Teal P: Antithrombotic and Thrombolytic Therapy for Ischemic Stroke: The Seventh ACCP Conference on Antithrombotic and Thrombolytic Therapy. Chest 2004, 126(3_suppl):483S-512. C:\Documents and Settings\David K. Cundiff\My Documents\Whistle\DVT\Chest AC Guidelines 9-04\AC for strokes Albers.htm

45. Eriksson BI, Bauer KA, Lassen MR, Turpie AGG: Fondaparinux Compared with Enoxaparin for the Prevention of Venous Thromboembolism after Hip-Fracture Surgery. N Engl J Med, 345(18):1298-1304.
http://content.nejm.org/cgi/content/abstract/345/18/1298

46. Bauer KA, Eriksson BI, Lassen MR, Turpie AGG: Fondaparinux Compared with Enoxaparin for the Prevention of Venous Thromboembolism after Elective Major Knee Surgery. N Engl J Med, 345(18):1305-1310.
http://content.nejm.org/cgi/content/abstract/345/18/1305

47. Lassen MR, Bauerb KA, Erikssonc BI, Turpie AG: Postoperative fondaparinux versus preoperative enoxaparin for prevention of venous thromboembolism in elective hip-replacement surgery: a randomised double-blind comparison. Lancet 2002, 359(9318):1715-1720.

48. Turpie AGG, Bauer KA, Eriksson BI, Lassen MR: Fondaparinux vs enoxaparin for the prevention of venous thromboembolism in major orthopedic surgery: A meta-analysis of 4 randomized double-blind studies. Arch Intern Med 2002, 162(16):1833-1840. http://archinte.ama-assn.org/cgi/content/full/162/16/1833?ijkey=1c22b7f98d6e9661f700253520c77cf9181873be

49. Agnelli G, Bergqvist D, Cohen AT, Gallus AS, Gent M: Randomized clinical trial of postoperative fondaparinux versus perioperative dalteparin for prevention of venous thromboembolism in high-risk abdominal surgery. PEGASUS investigators. Br J Surg. 2005, 92(10):1212-1220.

50. Buller HR, Davidson BL, Decousus H, Gallus A, Gent M, Piovella F, Prins MH, Raskob G, Segers AEM, Cariou R, Leeuwenkamp O, Lensing AWA: Fondaparinux or Enoxaparin for the Initial Treatment of Symptomatic Deep Venous Thrombosis: A Randomized Trial. Ann Intern Med 2004, 140(11):867-873
http://www.annals.org/cgi/reprint/140/811/867.pdf.
http://www.annals.org/cgi/content/abstract/140/11/867

51. The Matisse Investigators. Subcutaneous Fondaparinux versus Intravenous Unfractionated Heparin in the Initial Treatment of Pulmonary Embolism. N Engl J Med 2003, 349(18):1695-1702.
http://content.nejm.org/cgi/content/full/349/18/1695

References

52. Sanofi-Synthelabo to Sell to GlaxoSmithKline Arixtra(R), Fraxiparine(R) and Notre Dame de Bondeville Plant. PRNewswire-FirstCall. April 13, 2004. Accessed July 29, 2006.

53. Healy B. Who Says What's Best? US News & World Report. September 3, 2006. Available at: http://www.usnews.com/usnews/health/articles/060903/11healy.htm.

54. Cundiff DK: Evidence-based Medicine and the Cochrane Collaboration on Trial. MedGenMed, 9(2): http://medgenmed.medscape.com/viewarticle/557263 http://www.ncbi.nlm.nih.gov/pmc/articles/PMC1994886/?tool=pubmed.

55. Cundiff DK: A systematic review of Cochrane anticoagulation reviews. Medscape J Med 2009, 11(1):5. http://www.medscape.com/viewarticle/584084

56. 2nd ACCP Conference on Antithrombotic Therapy. American College of Chest Physicians. June 21, 1988. Proceedings. Chest 1989, 95(SUPPLEMENT):1 - 169.

57. The 3rd ACCP Conference on Antithrombotic and Thrombolytic Therapy. Chest 1995, 108(4 Suppl):1s -.

58. Hirsh J, Guyatt G, Albers GW, Schunemann HJ: The Seventh ACCP Conference on Antithrombotic and Thrombolytic Therapy: Evidence-Based Guidelines. Chest, 126(3_suppl):172S-173. http://www.chestjournal.org/cgi/reprint/126/3_suppl/172S

59. Antithrombotic and Thrombolytic Therapy: American College of Chest Physicians Evidence-Based Clincial Practice Guidelines (8th Edition). Chest, 133(no. 6 suppl):67S-968S. http://chestjournal.chestpubs.org/content/133/966_suppl/967S.full.

60. Hull RD, Feldstein W, Pineo GF, Raskob GE: Cost effectiveness of diagnosis of deep vein thrombosis in symptomatic patients. Thrombosis & Haemostasis 1995, 74(1):189-196.

61. Value of the ventilation/perfusion scan in acute pulmonary embolism. Results of the prospective investigation of pulmonary embolism diagnosis (PIOPED). The PIOPED Investigators. JAMA 1990, 263(20):2753-2759.

62. Heit JA: Venous Thromboembolism Epidemiology: Implications for Prevention and Management. SEMINARS IN THROMBOSIS AND HEMOSTASIS 2002, 28(supplement 2):3-14.

63. Hull RD, Feldstein W, Stein PD, Pineo GF: Cost-effectiveness of pulmonary embolism diagnosis. Archives of Internal Medicine 1996, 156(1):68-72.

64. Levine MN, Raskob G, Landefeld S, Kearon C: Hemorrhagic complications of anticoagulant treatment. Chest 1998, 114(5 Suppl):511S-523S.

65. Levine MN, Hirsh J, Landefeld S, Raskob G: Hemorrhagic complications of anticoagulant treatment. Chest 1992, 102(4 Suppl):352S-363S.

66. Landefeld CS, Beyth RJ: Anticoagulant-related bleeding: clinical epidemiology, prediction, and prevention. Am J Med 1993, 95(3):315-328.

67. Fihn SD, McDonell M, Martin D, Henikoff J, Vermes D, Kent D, White RH: Risk factors for complications of chronic anticoagulation. A multicenter study. Warfarin optimized outpatient follow-up study group. Ann Intern Med 1993, 118(7):511-520.

68. van der Meer FJ, Rosendaal FR, Vandenbroucke JP, Briet E: Bleeding complications in oral anticoagulant therapy. An analysis of risk factors. Arch Int Med 1993, 153(13):1557-1562.

69. Spencer FA, Lessard D, Emery C, Reed G, Goldberg RJ: Venous Thromboembolism in the Outpatient Setting. Arch Intern Med, 167(14):1471-1475. http://archinte.ama-assn.org/cgi/content/full/167/14/1471

70. McWilliam A, Lutter R, Nardinelli C. Health care savings from personalizing medicine using genetic testing: the case of warfarin.: AEI-Brookings Joint Center for Regulatory Studies, Working Paper; June 23, 2006.

71. Flaherty ML, Haverbusch M, Sekar P, Kissela BM, Kleindorfer D, Moomaw CJ, Broderick JP, Woo D: Location and Outcome of Anticoagulant-Associated Intracerebral Hemorrhage. Neurocrit. Care 2006, 5:197–201.

72. O'Brien CL, Gage BF: Costs and Effectiveness of Ximelagatran for Stroke Prophylaxis in Chronic Atrial Fibrillation. JAMA 2005, 293(6):699-706. http://jama.ama-assn.org/cgi/content/abstract/293/6/699

73. . National Health Expenditure Data. Centers for Medicare & Medicaid Services. Available at: http://www.cms.hhs.gov/NationalHealthExpendData/downloads/proj2009 .pdf. Accessed February 4, 2010.

74. Antithrombotics – current market and future outlook. IMS Health. June 2005. Available at: http://open.imshealth.com/webshop2/IMSinclude/i_article_20050630.asp and http://open.imshealth.com/webshop2/IMSinclude/%5C%5Copen.imshealth .com%5C. Accessed August 25, 2005.

75. Fanikos J, Grasso-Correnti N, Shah R, Kucher N, Goldhaber SZ: Major Bleeding Complications in a Specialized Anticoagulation Service. Am J Cardiol., 96(4):595-598.

76. Singer N. New Rivals to Warfarin as Blood Clot Preventer. NY Times. http://www.nytimes.com/2010/09/01/business/01drug.html?ref=health. August 31, 2010.

77. FDA Approves Pradaxa to Prevent Stroke in People With Atrial Fibrillation. Drugs.com. October 19, 2010. Available at:

References

http://www.drugs.com/newdrugs/fda-approves-pradaxa-prevent-stroke-atrial-fibrillation-2370.html.

78. Petersen JL, Mahaffey KW, Hasselblad V, Antman EM, Cohen M, Goodman SG, Langer A, Blazing MA, Le-Moigne-Amrani A, de Lemos JA, Nessel CC, Harrington RA, Ferguson JJ, Braunwald E, Califf RM: Efficacy and Bleeding Complications Among Patients Randomized to Enoxaparin or Unfractionated Heparin for Antithrombin Therapy in Non-ST-Segment Elevation Acute Coronary Syndromes: A Systematic Overview. JAMA, 292(1):89-96. http://jama.ama-assn.org/cgi/content/abstract/292/1/89

79. Rao SV, Jollis JG, Harrington RA, Granger CB, Newby LK, Armstrong PW, Moliterno DJ, Lindblad L, Pieper K, Topol EJ, Stamler JS, Califf RM: Relationship of Blood Transfusion and Clinical Outcomes in Patients With Acute Coronary Syndromes. JAMA 2004, 292(13):1555-1562. http://jama.ama-assn.org/cgi/content/abstract/292/13/1555

80. Moscucci M, Fox KAA, Cannon CP, Klein W, Lopez-Sendon J, Montalescot G, White K, Goldberg RJ, for the GRACE Investigators: Predictors of major bleeding in acute coronary syndromes: the Global Registry of Acute Coronary Events (GRACE). 10.1016/S0195-668X(03)00485-8. Eur Heart J, 24(20):1815-1823. http://eurheartj.oxfordjournals.org/cgi/content/abstract/24/20/1815

81. Segev A, Strauss BH, Tan M, Constance C, Langer A, Goodman SG; Canadian Acute Coronary Syndromes Registries Investigators.: Predictors and 1-year outcome of major bleeding in patients with non-ST-elevation acute coronary syndromes: insights from the Canadian Acute Coronary Syndrome Registries. Am Heart J. 2005, 150(4):690-694.

82. Eikelboom JW, Mehta SR, Anand SS, Xie C, Fox KAA, Yusuf S: Adverse Impact of Bleeding on Prognosis in Patients With Acute Coronary Syndromes. 10.1161/CIRCULATIONAHA.106.612812. Circulation, 114(8):774-782. http://circ.ahajournals.org/cgi/content/abstract/114/8/774

83. Leonardi MJ, McGory ML, Ko CY: The Rate of Bleeding Complications After Pharmacologic Deep Venous Thrombosis Prophylaxis: A Systematic Review of 33 Randomized Controlled Trials. 10.1001/archsurg.141.8.790. Arch Surg, 141(8):790-799. http://archsurg.ama-assn.org/cgi/content/abstract/141/8/790

84. Anderson FA, Jr. , Zayaruzny M, Heit JA, Fidan D, Cohen AT: Estimated annual numbers of US acute-care hospital patients at risk for venous thromboembolism. Am J Hematol, Epub ahead of print.

85. Goldhaber SZ: Venous thromboembolism risk among hospitalized patients: Magnitude of the risk is staggering. Am J Hematol 2007, 82(9):775-776.

86. Cundiff D, Agutter P, Malone P, Pezzullo J: Diet as prophylaxis and treatment for venous thromboembolism? Theoretical Biology and Medical Modelling 2010, (1):http://www.tbiomed.com/content/7/1/31.

87. McGarry LJ, Thompson D, Weinstein MC, Goldhaber SZ: Cost effectiveness of thromboprophylaxis with a low-molecular-weight heparin versus unfractionated heparin in acutely ill medical inpatients. Am J Manag Care 2004, 10(9):632-642. http://www.ajmc.com/Article.cfm?ID=2678&CFID=940752&CFTOKEN=67727289

88. Muntz J, Scott DA, Lloyd A, Egger M: Major bleeding rates after prophylaxis against venous thromboembolism: systematic review, meta-analysis, and cost implications. Int J Technol Assess Health Care. 2004, 20(4):405-414.

89. David Tovey. (Cochrane) Editor in Chief's response to a review by Dr David Cundiff in The Medscape Journal of Medicine. Cochrane Editorial Unit. April 21, 2010. Available at: http://www.editorial-unit.cochrane.org/editor-chiefs-response-review-dr-david-cundiff-medscape-journal-medicine.

90. Malone PC, Agutter PS. The Aetiology of Deep Venous Thrombosis: A Critical Historical and Epistemological Survey. Springer: Dordrecht; 2008.

91. Cundiff D, Agutter P, Malone P, Pezzullo J: Diet as prophylaxis and treatment for venous thromboembolism? Theoretical Biology and Medical Modelling 2010, (1):http://www.tbiomed.com/content/7/1/31/comments.

Chapter 14

1. Jeanne Lenzer, Shannon Brownlee. The Problem With Medicine: We Don't Know If Most of It Works. Discover Magazine. http://discovermagazine.com/2010/nov/11-the-problem-with-medicine-don.t-know-if-most-works.

2. Cundiff DK, Manyemba J, Pezzullo JC: Anticoagulants versus non-steroidal anti-inflammatories or placebo for treatment of venous thromboembolism. The Cochrane Database of Systematic Reviews 2006, Issue 1. Art. No.: CD003746. DOI: 10.1002/14651858.CD003746.pub2. http://www.mrw.interscience.wiley.com/cochrane/clsysrev/articles/CD003746/frame.html.

3. Standards for Developing Trustworthy Clinical Practice Guidelines (CPGs). Institute of Medicine. 3/23/2011. Available at: http://iom.edu/Reports/2011/Clinical-Practice-Guidelines-We-Can-Trust/Standards.aspx.

Acknowledgments

I owe huge debts of gratitude to many people that helped me over the 32 years—13 years of living and writing this book and those that helped me in the previous 19 years while I was employed by the LA County Department of Health Services.

Physicians that critiqued my work and encouraged me included William Lamers, MD (pioneering hospice physician), George Lundberg, MD (former chief editor of *JAMA* and the *Medscape Journal of Medicine*), Barbara Starfield, MD (Distinguished Professor of Public Health at the Johns Hopkins Medical School). Paul Agutter, MD, Colm Malone, MD, and John Pezzullo, PhD, coauthored a key evidence-based medicine article with me on anticoagulants in venous thromboembolism.

Graphic artist Eddie Young crafted a beautiful book cover.

My editor, Michele Fergus, worked incredible hours trying to make an impossible deadline. Jan Lundberg was also very helpful in guiding through the printing hurtles to bring the book to publication. Ralph Mattarochia assisted with publicity to bring the book to the attention of the media.

Family members that had to cope with and adapt to my ordeal included my daughters Amanda, Molly, and Chelsea, ex-wife Jenny.

The patients, nurses, interns and residents, faculty, and administrators of LA County + USC Medical Center gave me the experiences in palliative care, general internal medicine, and medical bureaucracy that helped form my perspective on the material in this book.

I dedicate the book to my patients that served as my teachers.

www.ingramcontent.com/pod-product-compliance
Lightning Source LLC
Chambersburg PA
CBHW060408220326
41598CB00023B/3068